ACADEMIC ENCOUNTERS

The *Academic Encounters* series uses authentic materials and a sustained content approach to teach students the academic skills they need to take college courses in English. There are two books in the series for each content focus: an *Academic Encounters* title and an *Academic Listening Encounters* title. As the series continues to grow, books at different levels and with different content area concentrations will be added. Please consult your catalog or contact your local sales representative for a current list of available titles.

Titles in the *Academic Encounters* series at publication:

Content Focus and Level	Components	*Academic Encounters*	*Academic Listening Encounters*
HUMAN BEHAVIOR High Intermediate to Low Advanced	Student's Book Teacher's Manual Audio Cassettes Audio CDs	ISBN 0 521 47658 5 ISBN 0 521 47660 7	ISBN 0 521 57821 3 ISBN 0 521 57820 5 ISBN 0 521 57819 1 ISBN 0 521 78357 7
LIFE IN SOCIETY Intermediate to High Intermediate	Student's Book Teacher's Manual Audio Cassettes Audio CDs	ISBN 0 521 66616 3 ISBN 0 521 66613 9	forthcoming forthcoming forthcoming forthcoming

Teacher's Manual

ACADEMIC ENCOUNTERS
LIFE IN SOCIETY

Reading
Study Skills
Writing

*Kristine Brown
& Susan Hood*

Intermediate to High Intermediate

CAMBRIDGE
UNIVERSITY PRESS

PUBLISHED BY THE PRESS SYNDICATE OF THE UNIVERSITY OF CAMBRIDGE
The Pitt Building, Trumpington Street, Cambridge, United Kingdom

CAMBRIDGE UNIVERSITY PRESS
The Edinburgh Building, Cambridge CB2 2RU, UK
40 West 20th Street, New York, NY 10011-4211, USA
477 Williamstown Road, Port Melbourne, VIC 3207, Australia
Ruiz de Alarcón 13, 28014 Madrid, Spain
Dock House, The Waterfront, Cape Town 8001, South Africa

http://www.cambridge.org

First published 2002

Printed in United States of America

Typeset in New Aster and Frutiger

A catalog record for this book is available from the British Library

Book design and layout services: Adventure House, NYC

Introduction

This Teacher's Manual provides specific teaching instructions for *Academic Encounters: Life in Society* and answers corresponding to its tasks. Photocopiable unit quizzes with answers are also included in this manual.

ABOUT *ACADEMIC ENCOUNTERS: LIFE IN SOCIETY*

Academic Encounters: Life in Society is a reading, study skills, and writing text based on material taken from sociology textbooks used in North American and other English-speaking colleges and universities. The student who will benefit most from this course will be at the intermediate to high-intermediate level of English-language proficiency. This student may well be encountering academic texts in English for the first time. However, the readings are short enough and the tasks sufficiently well scaffolded to allow a student at this level to access the texts successfully.

ABOUT THE *ACADEMIC ENCOUNTERS* SERIES

This content-based series is for nonnative speakers of English preparing to study in an English-speaking environment at the college or university level, and for native speakers of English who need to improve their academic skills for further study. The series consists of *Academic Encounters* books that help students improve their reading, study skills, and writing, and *Academic Listening Encounters* books that help students improve their listening, note-taking, and discussion skills. Each reading book corresponds in theme to a listening book, and each pair of theme-linked books focuses on an academic subject commonly taught in English-speaking colleges and universities. For example, *Academic Encounters: Life in Society* and *Academic Listening Encounters: Life in Society* both focus on sociology, whereas *Academic Encounters: Human Behavior* and *Academic Listening Encounters: Human Behavior* both focus on psychology and human communications. A reading book and a listening book with the same content focus may be used together to teach a complete four-skills course in English for Academic Purposes.

ANSWERS TO QUESTIONS COMMONLY ASKED ABOUT THE *ACADEMIC ENCOUNTERS* READING, STUDY SKILLS, AND WRITING BOOKS

Who are the books aimed at?

The *Academic Encounters* reading, study skills, and writing books are written for the student who has either just started or is about to start attending a college or university in an English-speaking environment. Ideally, this student should be entering an undergraduate program, although a graduate student who has never been exposed to academic English will also benefit from using these books. Even students who are native or nearly native speakers can benefit from the series, since the books prepare students for the types of texts and tasks that they will encounter in the college environment.

What approach is adopted and why?

In the *Academic Encounters* reading, study skills, and writing books, students are presented with authentic samples of text taken from textbooks used in English-speaking colleges and universities. The textbook material has been abridged and occasionally reorganized, but on the sentence level, little of the language has been changed. Students work with these texts to develop their reading and study skills. The high-interest content of the texts also provides stimulus for student writing assignments.

Academic Encounters adopts a content-based approach to the study of academic English. Students read through the authentic texts seemingly with the prime purpose of understanding the content. In fact, as students work through the book, they are also learning reading and study skills, and test-preparation strategies. Additionally, the texts are used for language study, so students become familiar with the vocabulary and sentence structures used in academic discourse.

Each unit of an *Academic Encounters* book focuses on some aspect of the book's content focus. The fact that the book has a unified thematic content throughout has several advantages. First, it gives the students a realistic sense of studying a course at a university, in which each week's assignments are related to and build on each other. Second, as language and concepts recur, the students begin to feel that the readings are getting easier, which helps to build their confidence as readers of academic text. Finally, after studying the book, some students may feel that they have enough background in the content focus area to take a course in that subject (for example, sociology) to fulfill part of their general education requirements.

How were the topics and readings chosen?

The topics and readings in each chapter were chosen for their appeal to students. It is important for students to be interested in what they are reading about and studying, and for them to be able to find personal connections to it. According to language acquisition theory, it can be argued that language development occurs more readily under such conditions. Similarly, it can be argued that the writing process is facilitated when students are well informed on a topic, have developed personal connections to it, and are engaged by it.

Are there many opportunities for student interaction?

Although the *Academic Encounters* reading, study skills, and writing books are centered on these skills, speaking activities abound. Students discuss the content of the texts before and after reading them; they often work collaboratively to solve task problems; they perform role-play activities; and they frequently compare answers in pairs or small groups.

How long does it take to teach an *Academic Encounters* reading, study skills, and writing book?

Each book contains five units of material. Each unit contains two chapters and each chapter requires approximately 8–10 hours of instruction. An *Academic Encounters* reading, study skills, and writing book could thus be suitable for a 64- to 80-hour course (when a teacher selects four of the five units) or an 80- to 100-hour course (when all the units are used). The book can be tailored to other time frames, however. For a shorter course, you might choose not to do every task in the book and to assign some tasks and texts as homework, rather than as classwork. For a longer course, you might choose to supplement the book with some content-related materials from your own files and to spend more time developing students' writing skills.

Do the units have to be taught in order?

The units do not have to be taught in the order in which they appear in the book, although this order is recommended. To a certain extent, tasks do build upon each other so that, for example, a note-taking task later in the book may draw upon information that has been presented in an earlier unit. However, if you want to teach the units out of order, you may do so. If this is the case, you might want to refer to the Task Index at the back of the book. This index lists all the tasks in the book and the page numbers on which they appear. It also indicates which tasks are preceded by a commentary box that provides useful tips and guidelines. If you teach the units out of order, you could review with your students any commentary boxes in skipped units that relate to tasks they are about to do.

What special design features does an *Academic Encounters* reading, study skills, and writing book have?

A great deal of attention has been paid to the design features in these books. There are two different types of pages: task pages and text pages. Tasks and texts never appear on the same page, and every new reading starts on a right-hand page faced by a left-hand page of prereading tasks. Task pages are clearly differentiated from text pages by a color bar running along the outside edge.

One of the most important design features of the book is that the text pages have been formatted to look very much like pages in a college-level textbook. The two-thirds' width column of text found in many textbooks has been employed, and there are figures, diagrams, and tables spread throughout the texts.

Photographs or illustrations with captions appear on almost every text page. Key words are shown in boldface and specialized terms are given in italics. The words in boldface also appear in the margin with brief definitions.

GENERAL GUIDELINES FOR TEACHING THE DIFFERENT COMPONENTS OF AN *ACADEMIC ENCOUNTERS* READING, STUDY SKILLS, AND WRITING BOOK

Each unit of an *Academic Encounters* reading, study skills, and writing book contains these elements:

- a unit title page
- a Previewing the Unit page
- two chapters, each containing four sections, each of which is divided into these parts:

  Preparing to Read
  Now Read
  After You Read

- two chapter writing assignments (one at the end of each chapter)
- a unit content quiz (photocopiable pages found in the teacher's manual only)

The remainder of this section contains guidelines for teaching each element. See Units 1–5 in the body of this Teacher's Manual for more detailed information, and for specific ideas for teaching each text and task found in *Academic Encounters: Life in Society*.

Unit title page

Each unit starts with a unit title page that contains the title of the unit, a large illustration or photograph that is suggestive of the content of the unit, and a brief paragraph that summarizes the unit. This page is intended to look like a typical unit opening page in a college or university course book.

Naturally, this page is a good place to start the study of a new unit. You should look at the title of the unit with the students and make sure they understand what it means. Then look at the picture and have students describe it and attempt to relate it to the title. Help students with vocabulary as necessary.

Finally, look at the summary paragraph at the bottom of the page. Read it to the students and check to be sure that they understand the vocabulary and key concepts. At this point, it is not necessary to introduce the unit topics in any depth, since the unit preview activities that follow will achieve this goal.

Previewing the unit

Following the unit title page is a two-page spread that includes, on the right-hand side, a contents page listing the titles of the two chapters in the unit and the titles of the four sections in each chapter. Again, this unit contents page resembles the typical chapter or unit contents page of a college textbook. On the left-hand page of the spread are tasks that relate to the titles on the unit contents page. These tasks preview the unit either by having students predict what information might be found in each section or by giving them some information from the unit and having them respond to it. In this way, students are given an overview of the unit before they start reading it in order to generate interest in the content of the unit. Furthermore, students are taught an important reading strategy, which is to preview the titles and headings of long readings.

Activities in "Previewing the Unit" are often to be done as pair work, followed by a report back to the whole class. The unit preview activities should take about one contact hour of class time to complete.

The chapters

Each unit is divided into two chapters, and each chapter contains four readings. Each reading forms the basis for a lesson, which should take approximately two contact hours to teach. There are three stages to the lesson, corresponding to the three headings on the task pages. First, students do a number of prereading tasks under the heading "Preparing to Read." Then students read the text, following the instruction under the heading "Now Read." Finally, students carry out a number of postreading tasks to be found under the heading "After You Read."

Preparing to Read

In an *Academic Encounters* reading, study skills, and writing book, prereading is regarded as a crucial step in the reading process. Thus, before students embark on reading any section of the book, they are required to do a page of prereading tasks, found on the left-hand page facing the first page of the reading.

Prereading activities serve three main functions:

1 They familiarize students with the content of the reading, arousing their interest and activating any knowledge that they may already have on the topic.

2 They introduce students to reading attack strategies, giving students tools to be used when they undertake any future reading assignments.

3 They expose students to some of the language in the text, making the text easier to process when students actually do the reading.

Each page of prereading tasks should take approximately 20 minutes of class time. Of course, some may require more or less time.

Although one or two prereading tasks are always included before each reading, you should look for ways to supplement these tasks with additional prereading activities. As you and your students work through the book, students become exposed to more and more prereading strategies. Having been introduced to these, students should be adding them to their repertoire, and you should encourage their regular use. For example, after having practiced the prereading strategies of examining graphic material, previewing headings, and skimming, students should ideally carry out these operations before each and every reading.

In general, the lower the level of the students' reading and overall language proficiency, the more important extensive prereading becomes. The more prereading tasks that are done, the easier it is for students to access the text when it comes time for them to do a closer reading.

Now Read

At the bottom of each "Preparing to Read" page is an instruction that tells the student to read the text. This is a deceptively simple instruction that raises an important question: How closely should the students read the text at this point? Some students, after doing prereading tasks such as skimming, believe that now they should read very slowly and carefully. But students should be discouraged from doing this. For one thing, it is a poor use of class time to have students poring silently over a text for 20 minutes or more, and more importantly it is vital that students at this level train themselves to read quickly, tolerating some ambiguity and going for understanding main ideas and overall text structure rather than every word and every detail.

To promote faster reading, the *Academic Encounters* reading, study skills, and writing books contain several speed-reading tasks, in which students try to put into operation techniques for faster reading. If students consistently apply these techniques, most texts will take between 3 and 7 minutes to read. Before students start reading any text, therefore, it is a good idea to give them a challenging time limit, within which they should aim to complete their reading of the text.

An alternative to doing every reading in class is to assign some of the longer readings as homework. When this is done, you should do the prereading task in class at the end of the lesson and then start the next class by having students quickly skim the text before moving on to the "After You Read" tasks.

After You Read

Sometimes, after having completed a text reading, the first order of business is not to move on to the "After You Read" tasks, but to revisit the "Preparing to Read" tasks to check to see if students had the correct answers in a predicting or skimming activity, for example.

Like the "Preparing to Read" tasks, the "After You Read" tasks are of many different types and serve several different functions. You should not expect to find many conventional reading comprehension tasks. Instead, students are often asked to demonstrate their understanding of a text in less direct ways, such as language focus, study skill, and test-preparation tasks. Each text in an *Academic Encounters* reading, study skills, and writing book is intended as an opportunity to develop a skill, not simply test comprehension.

Postreading tasks serve the following main functions:

1 They develop students' study skills repertoire by teaching them, for example, how to highlight a text, take notes in the margin or in notebooks, or guess the meaning of words in context.

2 They develop students' test-preparation skills, asking them to assess what they would need to do if they were going to be tested on the text.

3 They ask students to think about the content, to find a personal connection to it perhaps, or to apply new information in some way.

4 They highlight some of the most salient language in the text, either vocabulary or grammatical structures, and have students use that language in some way.

5 They have students read for meaning, look for main ideas, think critically about the text, or look for inferences.

6 They present students with a variety of different writing tasks, some of which may develop such key skills as summarizing and paraphrasing, others of which ask students to respond personally to the content of the reading.

Because the "After You Read" tasks do not always deal in detail with reading comprehension or language issues, some teachers may want to go back over the text, reading it to the students or along with the students, and picking out pieces of language that are worth drawing attention to and concepts that may not have been discussed.

The chapter writing assignments

Should you want your students to produce a longer piece of writing on the content of a chapter, each chapter ends with a choice of writing assignment topics. You are free to adopt any methodology you wish in having students write on these topics. No methodology is recommended in this book, although most contemporary writing teachers would probably espouse a multidraft approach with feedback on content for the early drafts, and feedback on language and writing mechanics for later drafts.

The content quizzes

At the back of this Teacher's Manual are five content quizzes, one for each unit. These are not mentioned anywhere in the student's book. The purpose of giving the students quizzes is to simulate what might happen in a college course. In college, students do not just read a text one day and never have to think about it again. Instead, they are expected to read, remember what they have read, and be able to demonstrate their understanding of a text under test conditions. The content quizzes provide these conditions. Furthermore, the quizzes force the students to revisit the texts and apply the reading and test preparation strategies taught in the book. The quizzes also give students practice in answering different types of test questions, since each quiz contains a mixture of true/false, multiple choice, short-answer, and short essay exam questions. Each quiz should take about 50 minutes of class time to complete, and the total score for each one is 100 points.

Belonging to a Group

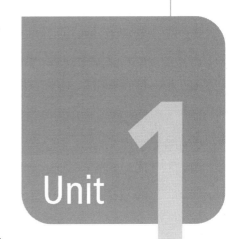

Unit 1

Unit title page (Student's Book pg. 1)

Make sure students understand the meaning of the unit title.
Ask them to look at the picture and think about how it relates to
the unit title.

Give students time to read the unit summary paragraph and check to make sure they
understand the areas the unit will cover. Be sure students understand that the focus is
on the influence of groups rather than on the groups themselves.

Previewing the unit (Student's Book pg. 2)

Draw students' attention to the task commentary box. Discuss the importance of
previewing for both understanding the content of a textbook unit or chapter, and for
understanding its organization.

Chapter 1: Marriage, Family, and the Home

1 After students have discussed the meanings of the terms with a partner, have them
share their understandings with the class. At this point, students may volunteer
information about types of families and households in their countries. Give a little
time to such a discussion, if it arises, but keep in mind that there is opportunity for
students to discuss this later in the chapter in "Thinking About the Topic" on page 4,
Task 4 on pages 8–9, and "Thinking About the Topic" on page 10.

2 Give students the opportunity to share both the child behaviors they have listed as
good and the methods of teaching these behaviors. Interesting and amusing
differences often arise with this topic if you have a culturally mixed class.

Chapter 2: The Power of the Group

1 After students have looked at and discussed the pictures, encourage them to talk
about why people do not do these things (if the behaviors are not common in their
country), or to talk about what groups in their country can be found playing chess,
shaking hands, or eating in the street.

2 You may need to prompt students to think beyond the obvious here. For example,
encourage them to think about their friends and acquaintances and consider through
what sorts of connections or activities they have gotten to know them. Some possible
responses may be family; church; neighborhood; school, college, or university; sports
or other interest group; gender; age; nationality; home town or city; urban or rural
origins; ethnicity or language.

Marriage, Family, and the Home

1 THE FAMILY TODAY

Preparing to read (Student's Book pg. 4)

THINKING ABOUT THE TOPIC

Discuss how thinking about the topic of a text before you read it helps you to understand the text. Encourage students to do this as a matter of course when they approach a new text.

Refer back to any discussion that occurred in "Previewing the Unit" about family and household groups in other countries. Encourage students to give details about typical families in their countries and to ask questions about each other's countries.

EXAMINING GRAPHIC MATERIAL

Discuss how previewing graphic material can help in understanding a text. The aim is not to understand the graph fully, but to get a general idea of what it is about.

This is a good opportunity to introduce terms to describe different types of graphs and their parts, for example, line graph, bar graph, vertical axis, horizontal axis, etc.

Answers

Fig 1.2	**a**
Fig 1.3	**b**
Fig 1.1	**c**

Now read

Refer to page xi of this Teacher's Manual for suggestions about ways in which students can read the text.

Task 1 READING FOR THE MAIN IDEA

Emphasize the importance of this skill, and encourage students to use the two strategies listed in the task commentary box. Stress that students need to choose the sentence that captures the whole idea of the text and reflects all parts of the text to some degree.

After students have chosen an answer, go through each choice and elicit from them why it is or is not the best statement of the main idea.

Answer

a

Task 2 BUILDING VOCABULARY: DEALING WITH UNKNOWN WORDS

1,2 | The aim is to review what students know about deducing meanings of unknown words and to introduce new strategies. Ensure that students understand what each strategy in the skills box means. Encourage students also to make use of their general knowledge when reading. For example, students might know from their general knowledge and experience that when couples divorce, they often go to court to determine which of them will become the main parent to care for the children. With this knowledge, they may then deduce the meaning of *custody*.

Sample answers

significantly: in an important way
   (from the context and from general knowledge; also from knowledge of the word *sign*, which has a sense of showing something clearly)
conflict: disagreement, quarreling
   (from the context) (Students might mention other words beginning with *con*, for example, *contrast* or *contest*, that have a sense of "opposing." Most *con* words, however, have the meaning of "with" or "together," for example, *conspiracy* or *construct*.)
households: people who live together as a group in a house
   (from knowledge of the word *house*; from the overall context)
poverty: state of being poor
   (from the context – the whole paragraph – and from general knowledge)
custody: care and responsibility for someone
   (definition given in the text in parentheses; also from context and general knowledge)
discipline: setting rules about behavior and making sure they are followed
   (from the example given within the context)

Task 3 LANGUAGE FOCUS: WRITING ABOUT CHANGES

1 | **Sample answers**
   • "new forms of the family unit have become increasingly common." (par. 1)
   • "there has been a tremendous increase in the numbers of married women. . . ." (par. 2)
   • "The employment of married women has increased family income significantly . . . ." (par. 3)
   • "there has been a huge rise in the number of children growing up . . . ." (par. 4)
   • ". . .the proportion of single-parent families in the United States more than doubled. . . ." (par. 4)
   • "stepfamilies have also become quite common." (par. 7)

Students may comment on the graph publication dates and the latest year for which they give information. Explain to students that not all statistics are updated regularly or at the same time. Students will come across many statistics in the texts and in graphs and charts in this book. The dates of these vary to some extent, but in all cases the graphs and charts provide the most accurate information available at the time of publication.

It can be useful to have students write their sentences on overhead transparencies. You can then discuss and make any needed changes to the sentences.

Task 4 READING ACTIVELY

This is an aspect of reading that is often overlooked. Students need to be reminded to take time out from close reading of words and sentences to think about and question what they are reading. They could talk to another student about their ideas, or write comments and questions in the margins of the text or in their notes. Assure students that the more they do this, the better they will remember what they have read.

1,2 The two steps here require students to talk about their responses to the text. Tell students that they should always think about and question what they are reading, even when they are not in a classroom situation.

Encourage students to talk as much as possible in this activity.

2 ALTERNATIVE LIFESTYLES

Preparing to read (Student's Book pg. 10)

THINKING ABOUT THE TOPIC

Be sure you talk about the concept of the acceptability of the lifestyles listed. The discussion should go beyond whether or not these lifestyles exist in the students' countries to the reasons why they do or do not. Encourage as much discussion as possible. Even if the class is a single nationality group, it will be interesting for them to discuss the frequency and acceptability of these lifestyles. There may well be differences from one part of the country to another, or from urban to rural areas.

Help students to think about how common these lifestyles are in the United States (or another English-speaking country) based on their own personal experience and what they know from the media.

SKIMMING

Have your students read the task commentary box. Make the point that this skill is important whether reading in your first or second language. Encourage them to use this strategy whenever they read, even if not explicitly told to do so.

Draw particular attention to the importance of reading the introductory paragraph when skimming. Students should read it quickly, not taking time concentrating on words they do not know, but getting a general idea of the text's content.

1,2	Be sure that students keep to the 1-minute time limit in both steps. Have them close or turn over their books at the end of each minute's skimming.
3	Go over the different ways that introductions help us to understand texts, using the four statements a–d, before asking students to identify the function of this particular introduction.

Answer

a

Now read

Refer to page xi of this Teacher's Manual for suggestions about ways in which students can read the text.

After you read (Student's Book pg. 13)

Task 1 READING BOXED TEXTS

Go over the information in the task commentary box. Ask students whether they have seen boxed texts elsewhere. If you have a magazine or newspaper on hand, you could show them an example.

1	Tell students that reading boxed texts can be a good way to ease into reading a text that has lots of information. Boxed texts are usually short and self-contained and give the reader an idea of a topic that is in the main text.
2	**Answer** give a definition or definitions, and/or give an interesting example of the idea of *alternative lifestyles* in the main text

Task 2 BUILDING VOCABULARY: USING KNOWLEDGE OF RELATED WORDS

Read through the task commentary box with your students. Refer back to Task 2 on page 7 of the Student's Book, which gives an overview of how to work out meanings of unknown words.

1	You might prefer to have the students do this step in pairs so they can share their knowledge.

Sample answers

independent: depend, dependent, independence
formal: form, formula, format
sociological: society, social, sociology, logic, logical; other -*ology* and -*ological* words
ideals: idea
mainstream: main, stream
serial: series

2	After students have checked the meanings in their dictionaries, you might ask them what other related words they found.

Task 3 NOTE TAKING

Read through the task commentary box with students. Discuss how easy or difficult they find note taking. Ask them about abbreviations they usually use and write them up on the board.

1 | Read the notes and make sure that students understand them. Have students look back at the original text to identify what the note taker has left out of the notes and what he/she has included. Ask them if they would have included any other details.

2 | Have students do this step independently.

Sample answers
Staying single
• huge incr in last 20 yrs
• 1998, <u>10%</u> lived alone (Austr.) – <u>25%</u> of all households (U.S.)
• most <u>in late 20s</u>
• reasons given – <u>not met right person; marr – too much commit & respons; or prefer sgle lifestyle</u>
• 2 sociological reasons – 1) <u>decline in soc pressure to get married</u>, 2) opps for singles to have good life incr'd esp for women

3 | **Sample answers**
Communal living (*communes*)
• share possns & skills – indep. mainstr soc
• for ex., grow own food, educ chn
• 1000s arnd world – var size & type
• concept now applied to city housing – *cohousing*
• for ex., Sacramento – share gdns, din rm, etc
• like big family

Task 4 TEST TAKING: PREPARING FOR A SHORT-ANSWER QUIZ

Ask students if they have ever tried to prepare for a quiz by trying to predict the questions. Lead the students through the task commentary box, making sure that they understand each type of quiz question.

1 | After students do this step, discuss their answers to the questions.

2 | **Answers**
   1 Type 1
   2 Type 2
   3 Type 3

3 | Encourage each pair of students to write at least one of the more difficult Type 3 questions.

4 | Make sure that students use this opportunity to practice their oral skills.

5,6 | The focus here is on Type 3 questions that take readers beyond the text and ask them to reflect on the data in a critical way. Tell students that their critical judgments must be supported with good reasons.

3 HOW WE LEARN TO BEHAVE

Preparing to read (Student's Book pg. 16)

PREDICTING
Discuss with students the importance of predicting in the reading process. Make the point that predicting is something that they should be doing *while* they read as well as *before* they read, that is, predicting what is to come after each heading, each paragraph, and each page.

Encourage students to come up with as many ideas as possible and not to worry about understanding the terms used in the headings exactly. The focus of this task is on the process.

After students have read the text more carefully in the "Now Read" section, refer back to their predictions, confirming or clarifying their ideas.

PERSONALIZING THE TOPIC
Discuss with students why it is easier to understand and remember information with which we can make a personal connection.

As students discuss the five situations in groups, circulate among them, noting their ideas and helping them as needed with language. At the end of their discussions, have students report on their solutions and reasons.

Now read

Refer to page xi of this Teacher's Manual for suggestions about ways in which students can read the text.

After you read (Student's Book pg. 19)

Task 1 LANGUAGE FOCUS: DEFINING
Definitions can be difficult to write so it is worth drawing students' attention to how they are constructed in the texts they read.

1 | Draw students' attention to the fourth sentence, which defines *negative sanctions*. This sentence uses two ways of defining the term – a synonym in parentheses and the verb *mean*.

Answers
2 (Sanctions) are consequences following a behavior that influence whether the behavior will be repeated.

3 (Positive sanctions) mean that the behavior is followed by something that is a reward.

4 (Negative sanctions) (also known as punishments) mean that something bad happens after a behavior occurs.

5 (Modeling) refers to learning by watching the behavior of others – especially parents – and copying that behavior.

2 Make sure students look back at the context in which these terms occurred in the text to help them write their definitions. Write some students' sentences on the board (try to get a range of defining patterns) and discuss.

Task 2 BUILDING VOCABULARY: LEARNING WORDS RELATED TO THE TOPIC

Discuss the usefulness of this strategy as a way to expand vocabulary.

1,2 If any interesting differences arise because of cross-cultural differences in child-rearing, discuss them with students. Refer back to the discussion of good behavior in children in "Previewing the Unit," Chapter 1, on page 2 of the Student's Book if relevant. You could extend the activity with more adjectives if you wish.

Answers

Positive sanctions: *polite, neat, well-behaved, respectful, responsible, caring, kind, cheerful, obedient*

Negative sanctions: *rebellious, resentful, rude, aggressive, disobedient, selfish, cruel*

Task 3 SUMMARIZING

Read through the task commentary box with students. Draw their attention to the importance of summarizing when writing essays and reports.

Answers

Socialization is the <u>process</u> of learning how to behave in the society we live in. The job of socialization is performed by several groups called <u>socializing agents</u> . The family, the school, and the peer group are the most important socializing agents, and of these three, the <u>family</u> is the most important, especially in the early years. Two important ways that families and other socializing agents teach children to behave are <u>sanctions</u> and <u>modeling</u>. Sanctions are the <u>consequences</u> that follow a particular behavior and influence whether or not the behavior will be <u>repeated</u>. Sanctions can be positive (<u>rewards</u>) or negative (punishments). Modeling is learning by <u>watching</u> the behavior of others – especially parents – and copying that behavior. Children are socialized differently depending on the <u>culture</u> they are brought up in.

Task 4 APPLYING WHAT YOU READ

Discuss with students how thinking of ways to apply their new knowledge will make it easier to remember as well as to deepen their understanding of the text.

1 Ask students if they are aware of advice columns in magazines and newspapers, and if they ever read them. Encourage as much as discussion as possible.

2 Give students help with structuring their letters, if needed. For example, letters from advice columnists usually begin by referring to the problem, then show sympathetic understanding of the problem, and, finally, offer advice about what to do. Letters should be no more than two paragraphs.

4 THE IMPORTANCE OF THE SOCIAL ENVIRONMENT

Preparing to read (Student's Book pg. 22)

THINKING ABOUT THE TOPIC

1 | Make sure students understand the meaning of each characteristic in the chart. Make it clear that social environment includes the home environment, in other words, the way in which parents bring up children.

2 | Students are likely to find it difficult sometimes to decide which column to check. This does not matter as long as it gives rise to discussion about why it was difficult. After students have discussed their choices in groups, ask them to share with the class any interesting findings or examples.

3 | Encourage students to see skimming the text as an automatic part of their reading process, to be done whether or not they are asked to do so.

Now read

Refer to page xi of this Teacher's Manual for suggestions about ways in which students can read the text.

After you read (Student's Book pg. 25)

Task 1 VISUALIZING PARTS OF THE TEXT
Discuss how helpful photographs and drawings are when we read, and how imagining visual images when they are not provided can also help us.

Answers

1 Anna

2 the wild boy of Aveyron

3 Edith

4 infant in orphanage

Task 2 BUILDING VOCABULARY: USING CONTEXT CLUES
Discuss the importance of this skill when reading. Emphasize the idea of being satisfied with gaining a general meaning of the unknown words, of not always having to have precise meanings.

1,2 | Remind students to also use their general knowledge of a topic as a tool in figuring out the meaning of a word.

Answers

1 traits

(Clues are examples in the same sentence, such as, *skin color*, and in following sentences, *active* and *nervous*.)

2 passive

(Clue is given by the parallel structure of two sentences about temperamental opposites – *passive*, the first trait in the second sentence, parallels *active*, the first trait in the first sentence.)

3 enhanced

(Clues are given by opposition to *restricted* and by general topic of paragraph.)

4 outraged

(Clue is given by second clause in the sentence: "and did not want to have anything to do with the child.")

5 orphanage

(Clue is given by descriptive clause "where 18-month-old infants were left lying on their backs in tiny rooms most of the day without any human contact.")

6 impaired

(Clues are given in the two sentences that follow. Another clue is the term *harmful effects* in the first sentence.)

7 survived

(Clues are from the opposing focus in the preceding sentence, specifically the phrase "children died.")

8 skipped

(Clues are from clauses which precede and follow: "finished grammar school in four years" and "and went straight to college;" and from ages mentioned in the following sentence.)

Task 3 READING FOR MAIN IDEAS

Discuss how crucial this reading skill is for effective study. It is very easy for students, when faced with long and complex texts, to lose sight of what the main focus of the text is.

1 | This step focuses on the simplest aspect of the skill – identifying topics of paragraphs. Students should do this as quickly as possible.

Answers

2 paragraph 5

3 paragraph 1

4 paragraph 6

5 paragraph 7

6 paragraph 2

7 paragraph 8

8 paragraph 4

2 | This step is more difficult. All the sentences express ideas in the text, but only one captures the overall sense.

Answer
Sentence **c** is correct because it captures the general ideas in paragraphs 1–3 and the two types of examples that illustrate the ideas in paragraphs 4–8.
Sentence **a** only reflects paragraphs 1–3; sentence **b** only reflects paragraph 2; sentence **d** captures the main idea but excludes the examples of specialized socialization in paragraphs 7 and 8.

Task 4 CITING STUDIES IN YOUR WRITING
Explain the concept of *citation* and contrast it with *quotation*. Write the formulaic pattern in the task commentary box on the board, and explain it.

1 | Point out to students that this sentence is also an excellent example of a one-sentence summary, a skill they will practice further in Task 1, "Writing a One-Sentence Summary," in Chapter 3, section 3, "After You Read" on page 69 of the Student's Book.

2 | There are a number of ways to do the citation and various aspects of the research to focus on.

Sample answers
In his study of children brought up in orphanages, Rene Spitz (1945) found that infants who received little attention suffered harmful effects similar to those experienced by other socially deprived children.

In his study of infants in orphanages, Rene Spitz (1945) found that more than a third of the infants who were deprived of human contact for very long periods did not survive for more than three years.

In his study of infants living in orphanages, Rene Spitz (1945) found that children who were left alone for very long periods were impaired in every possible way.

3 | You might want to limit students' choice to particular texts or examples.

Chapter 1 WRITING ASSIGNMENT (Student's Book pg. 27)

Although no particular writing methodology is recommended in this book, each chapter writing assignment is a good opportunity to review with students whichever writing strategies you want them to use. Some examples include brainstorming, writing an outline, writing an introductory paragraph that introduces the topic and the ideas to be developed, and checking their work for spelling and grammar. In a multidraft approach, students can work in pairs to give each other feedback – first for content and later for grammar and mechanics. You may also want to let students share their completed work with classmates. This provides them with the experience of writing for a *real* audience, which can be a valuable motivating tool. Depending on the writing process your students will follow, you may want to assign part or all of the process as homework.

Read through the topics with your students, eliciting from them which texts might be helpful to review prior to writing about each topic.

In some chapters, students will have done writing or note-taking tasks prior to the chapter writing assignment. In such cases, have students review the work they have already done to see if it would be useful in relation to any of the topics in the chapter writing assignment.

You may want to put students who are going to write about the same topic in pairs or small groups to brainstorm ideas before they write and to give each other feedback afterwards.

Chapter 2

The power of the group

1 THE INFLUENCE OF CULTURE

Preparing to read (Student's Book pg. 28)

THINKING ABOUT THE TOPIC

1 | Make sure that students understand the meaning of *norms* as rules about acceptable and unacceptable behavior in different cultural groups. Have students do this step individually because they need to think about the rating scale.

2,3 | Encourage as much discussion as possible.

Now read

Refer to page xi of this Teacher's Manual for suggestions about ways in which students can read the text.

After you read (Student's Book pg. 32)

Task 1 UNDERSTANDING KEY TERMS IN THE TEXT

Discuss how in academic reading students will come across many new technical terms, and how it is usually important to understand these terms precisely. Explain that finding examples of the terms can be the best way to understand and then remember meanings.

Task 2 WRITING EXPANDED DEFINITIONS

1 | Give students time to study the example and then discuss any questions.

2 | Refer students back to Task 1, on page 19 of the Student's Book, which presents language that is useful for writing definitions.

Sample answers

The terms are clearly defined in the text, but you can encourage students to use their own wording as well as wording from the text. The following sample definitions are not worded in the same way as those in the text:

- *Values* are socially shared ideas about what is good, desirable, or important.

- *Norms* are rules about what is socially acceptable and unacceptable.

- *Folkways* are less serious kinds of norms.

- *Taboos* are very strong norms that forbid a certain activity or behavior.

- *Mores* are norms that provide standards for moral behavior.

3 | Discuss phrases students can use to link their definition to examples, such as the following:

such as, . . .	one example is . . .
another example is . . .	one way this happens is . . .

Task 3 READING BOXED TEXTS

There is likely to be a lively and humorous discussion of kissing rules. Encourage students to ask each other questions about how and why these rules came about, and how and why they might be changing.

Task 4 APPLYING WHAT YOU READ

Students will probably express varying opinions on acceptable and unacceptable classroom behavior. Be sure to keep them focused on trying to develop rules that are acceptable to all.

2 PEER GROUP PRESSURE

Preparing to read (Student's Book pg. 34)

PERSONALIZING THE TOPIC

Discussions here will vary depending on the age of students. If students are still adolescents, encourage them to think about young people in early adolescence, and how young adolescents might be different from them. Encourage discussion of adolescence in different cultures. You could stimulate discussion by bringing in a few magazines or photographs showing current teen idols, fashions, and behaviors.

PREVIEWING ART IN THE TEXT

Ask students if they generally look at photographs, artwork, and captions when they read and in what situations they use this strategy. Discuss the fact that photographs and other art are usually chosen to reflect the main or important ideas in a text and, thus, are a good guide to its meaning.

1,2 | Make sure students look back at their sentences after reading the text.

Now read

Refer to page xi of this Teacher's Manual for suggestions about ways in which students can read the text.

After you read (Student's Book pg. 36)

Task 1 SHORT-ANSWER QUIZZES: MAKING USE OF YOUR OWN EXPERIENCE

1,2 | **Answers**

 1 any one of the following: to be independent from adult authorities; social skills – how to get along with others; the value of friendship among equals

 2 any three of the following: believe the same things; talk the same way; dress the same way; listen to the same music; like and dislike the same TV stars and celebrities

 3 any two of the following: financial matters; educational matters; career and other serious matters

 4 social activities such as which boy or girl to date and what clubs to join

 5 less important because they become more independent and start to adopt adult values such as wanting to get good grades and good jobs

Task 2 VARYING YOUR LANGUAGE

Discuss the task commentary box and make the point that it is important to recognize when writers are referring to the same ideas using different words. Explain that writers do this to give variety to their writing.

1 | **Answers**
 • young people: children, students, the adolescent peer group, teenagers, adolescents, youngsters, peers, peer group members, early adolescents

 • adults: parents, teachers, adult authorities, older people, mothers and fathers

 • be likely to: tend to, frequently, are inclined to, are more likely to, tend more to

2 | **Sample answers**
 • people who are over 65: elderly people, the elderly, older people, senior citizens, retired people, the older generation, grandmothers and grandfathers, grandparents

 • babies: infants, little ones, newborns

- children under 5: preschoolers, toddlers, small children
- people in paid employment (people who work): employed people, workers, people in the workforce, the workforce

Task 3 LANGUAGE FOCUS: WRITING ABOUT DIFFERENCES

1 | Make sure that students understand that the sentence structures 1–4 are basic patterns. For example, the structure "There is a difference between X and Y" also includes the sentences "There may be a difference between X and Y" and "There is a huge difference between X and Y."

2 | **Answers**

(Adolescents and adults are different in) many ways. (Teenagers differ from adults,) (for example, in the way) they handle finances. (Teenagers are likely to) spend all their money as soon as they receive it, (whereas most adults try to) save some of their money for future expenses. (There is also a difference in) what adults and adolescents spend their money on. (Young people tend to) spend their money on the things they want – music, movies, going out – (whereas older people are more) (likely to) spend it on the things they need – clothes, food, housing.

3 | Have students begin their paragraph with a general statement about the differences between the two groups in the area chosen, and then give examples using the various sentence patterns shown in step 1.

3 CROWDS

Preparing to read (Student's Book pg. 38)

THINKING ABOUT THE TOPIC

1 | Encourage students to go beyond the obvious observation that the people are in a crowd. Elicit what being in any crowd is like, for example, what you do, what others do, how you feel.

2 | Encourage students to focus on the differences in atmosphere, purpose, the behavior of the people, and what could happen as a result of their behavior.

3 | Encourage as much discussion as possible. Be sensitive to the fact that in some countries government regulations about people gathering as a crowd may exist. Students may or may not feel comfortable about talking about these regulations.

SKIMMING: READING FIRST SENTENCES

Discuss the task commentary box and emphasize the usefulness of this strategy when dealing with academic texts.

Encourage students to do the task without looking further than the first sentence of each paragraph to check their ideas. It is important that they do it based on the first sentences.

Answers

a paragraph 2

b paragraph 5

c paragraph 1

d paragraph 4

e paragraph 3

f paragraphs 6 and 7

Now read

Refer to page xi of this Teacher's Manual for suggestions about ways in which students can read the text.

After you read (Student's Book pg. 41)

Task 1 APPLYING WHAT YOU READ

1 | Refer back to the discussion of crowd scenes in "Thinking About the Topic" on page 38. Remind students of some of the differences discussed then. Give students time to do the task individually because they will have to read paragraph 5 of the text closely, and then think about the best classification.

Answers

1 casual

2 conventional

3 acting

4 acting

5 casual

6 expressive

7 acting

8 acting

2 | Some crowds are difficult to classify because they lie somewhere in between the four classes identified by Blumer. It is likely, therefore, that there will be differences of opinion on some items. Encourage as much discussion as possible of the reasons for students' classifications.

3,4 | Give students time to think about their experience and to fill in the chart, but devote the most time to the pair discussion of their responses. Encourage students to ask questions about each other's experiences. If time allows, ask them to share any particularly unusual or interesting crowd experiences with the class.

5 Refer students back to paragraphs 6 and 7 in which the two theories are discussed; give students time to read them again. Ask a volunteer to state what the essence of each theory is. Be sure that the volunteer's explanation makes the differences between the two theories clear to all. Encourage as much discussion as possible.

Task 2 LANGUAGE FOCUS: TOPIC SENTENCES

Discuss the importance of topic sentences in reading and writing academic texts. Explain that topic sentences are not used in all types of writing. For example, they are not always used in newspaper articles or narratives. Remind students of the usefulness of topic sentences when skimming.

1 **Answers**

The first sentence of each paragraph is a topic sentence. However, you should note the following:

- par. 2: It could be argued that the topic sentence is the second sentence, and the first sentence functions as a link between this paragraph and the preceding one.

- par. 3: It could be argued that the second sentence is really the topic sentence because it is the answer to the question in the first sentence. Explain to students that very often the second sentence of a paragraph will restate, elaborate, or amplify the first sentence and, in so doing, will establish firmly the topic of a paragraph.

- Ask for volunteers to explain which phrases or sentences in the text of each paragraph led them to decide which sentence was the topic sentence. If any students got wrong answers, be sure they understand why their answers are wrong and why the correct answers are right.

2 **Answers**

1 b

2 c

3 a

Task 3 BUILDING VOCABULARY: USING GRAMMAR TO WORK OUT UNKNOWN WORDS

Discuss the task commentary box and, if necessary, review the parts of speech.

1,2 **Answers**

relatively: adverb modifying the adjectives *unorganized*, *spontaneous*, and *unpredictable*
spontaneous: adjective qualifying the noun *behavior*
masses: noun
temporarily: adverb modifying the verb *doing*
traits: noun
emerges: verb
rioters: noun
primitive: adjective qualifying the noun *side*
irrational: adjective relating to *us*

4 PANIC!

Preparing to read (Student's Book pg. 44)

PERSONALIZING THE TOPIC

1-3 | Encourage students to give details of their reactions and the reasons for their rankings. Students may need some help with language to describe feelings of fear. You might like to introduce expressions such as *heart in one's mouth*, *stomach churning*, or *heart stopped*.

Now read

Refer to page xi of this Teacher's Manual for suggestions about ways in which students can read the text.

After you read (Student's Book pg. 47)

Task 1 SCANNING

Read through the task commentary box with your students and discuss the importance of scanning. Be sure they understand the distinction between scanning and skimming.

Answers

1 *panic* (an extreme type of collective behavior): "a useless response to a serious threat or danger" (par. 4)

2 any two of the four conditions mentioned in paragraph 5

3 *mass hysteria*: "when numerous people engage in wild or frenzied activity without checking the source of their fear" (par. 6)

Task 2 UNDERSTANDING COMPLEX SENTENCES

Have students read through the task commentary box. Emphasize the importance of understanding complex sentences in order to gain a thorough understanding of academic texts. The skill of understanding the structure of complex sentences is one that challenges students significantly when reading, and often gets little attention as we encourage students to accept general meaning and not worry too much about parts they do not understand. It is important to recognize that often students do need to understand the exact meaning, and to do this, they need to be able to see how all the parts of a sentence work together to make meaning. Other tasks you might give students to help them practice this skill are underlining main clauses in multiclause sentences or drawing an arrow between each subject and its verb(s).

1 | Explain to students that there are often different ways that sentences can be broken up into meaning units, but that some words must go together such as verbs and adverbs, or nouns and adjectives. Explain that good punctuation helps us to understand and break up sentences into meaning units, which is something students should keep in mind when they write.

Sample answers

1 The people / in the Iroquois Theater / and the Mecca tunnel / behaved / as people often do / when faced with unexpected and dangerous situations / such as fires, earthquakes, and floods: / they panicked.

2 This fear / is made worse / if the people involved / think / they will be trapped / or unable to escape.

3 Typically / these are / people / whose desire to save themselves / makes them ignore / the fate of others / and of the dangerous consequences / of their panic.

4 This is when / numerous people / engage in / wild or frenzied activity / without checking / the source of their fear.

3 | How students explain their answers will depend to some extent on their grasp of grammatical terms. If students are not experienced with these terms, avoid getting bogged down in explanations and be ready to accept explanations of their divisions that make good sense.

Task 3 BUILDING VOCABULARY: WORD MAPS FOR REMEMBERING NEW VOCABULARY

Encourage students to make use of this strategy when entering words in a vocabulary notebook.

1,2 | Circulate among students while they are doing these steps and take note of any especially interesting words or of any misuse of vocabulary. Discuss these with the class, perhaps adding some examples of your own.

Task 4 WRITING A LISTING PARAGRAPH

Lead students through the commentary box. Explain that this organizational pattern is perhaps the most straightforward and useful one for them to understand and to use in their writing.

1 | **Sample answer**

(Paragraph 5 is the listing paragraph.)
Conditions for panic:
1. people believe there is a serious danger
2. intense fear of the danger
3. individuals with natural tendency to panic
4. people increase terror by words and actions
5. lack of cooperation

2,3 | Refer back to the situations discussed in "Personalizing the Topic" on page 44 of the Student's Book. You might model the writing process using the situation that you found the most frightening.

Chapter 2 WRITING ASSIGNMENT (Student's Book pg. 50)

Read through the topics with your students, eliciting from them which texts might be helpful to review prior to writing about each topic. You may want to put students who are going to write about the same topic in pairs or small groups to brainstorm ideas before they write and to give each other feedback afterwards.

Refer to the discussion of the Chapter 1 Writing Assignment on page 11 of this Teacher's Manual for further suggestions.

Gender and Sexuality

Unit Title Page (Student's Book pg. 51)

Be prepared to deal with questions about the meanings of *gender* and *sexuality*, if they arise. *Gender* refers to the classification of human beings according to whether they are male or female. Sometimes the words *gender* and *sex* are used interchangeably. *Gender* is more often used to talk about socially conditioned typical behavior of males and females; *sex* is more often used to talk about physical characteristics. Sometimes *gender* is used rather than *sex* because of the latter's meaning of *sexual relations*. *Sexuality* refers to a person's ability to experience or express sexual feelings. For example, we can talk about a teenager's developing *sexuality*. It is also used to mean a person's sexual preference or orientation, for example, heterosexual, homosexual, or bisexual.

Elicit ideas about what the major influences on gender roles might be and what the current gender issues are regarding men, women, home, and work.

Previewing the unit (Student's Book pg. 52)

Give students a minute to look at the Unit Contents page (Student's Book pg. 53). Have them predict some ideas that might be found in each section of the two chapters.

Chapter 3: Growing Up Male or Female

Try to group the students so that there is a mixture of cultural backgrounds. Ask one student from each group to report on some of the differences that were discussed.

Chapter 4: Gender Issues Today

1 The survey was conducted through a telephone poll of 505 Americans aged 18 to 24. The results mean that 30% of the women polled said it was easier to be a woman, and 59% said it was easier to be a man. Presumably, 11% were unsure, though this is not mentioned. Of the males polled, 21% said it was easier to be a woman, and 65% said it was easier to be a male. Again, presumably, the remaining 14% did not give a definite answer.

2 Encourage students to explain the reasons for their responses.

3 If possible, have students survey students in other classes during a class break. Make sure students record whether the answer was from a man or a woman. Writing on this topic is one of the choices for the Chapter 4 Writing Assignment, so make sure students keep their results for possible use at that point.

4 Tally the class results of the survey on the board. Discuss how they compare with the survey results given in step 1.

Growing Up Male or Female

1 BRINGING UP BOYS AND GIRLS

Preparing to read (Student's Book pg. 54)

SKIMMING
Answer
a

PERSONALIZING THE TOPIC
Encourage as much discussion as possible. For questions 3 and 5, encourage students to give reasons for their opinions. Draw students' attention to any patterns that emerge. For example, do female students have different attitudes about the toys than male students?

Now read

Refer to page xi of this Teacher's Manual for suggestions about ways in which students can read the text.

After you read (Student's Book pg. 57)

Task 1 NOTE TAKING: MAKING A CHART
Read through the task commentary box with your students. Make sure they understand that a chart is particularly useful when taking notes from a comparison-contrast text or a text that includes comparison/contrast sections. It is also useful with cause and effect texts or texts organized chronologically.

1 Sample answers

	Girls	Boys
Color of clothing	pink	blue
Way children are handled	handled gently cuddled and kissed	bounced around and lifted high in the air
Types of toys children are given	dolls	cars, trucks, and building blocks
Amount of attention paid by parents to appearance	Mothers think about how pretty girls should look	not so much
Language and conversation learned from parents	talk about feelings talk politely	don't talk about feelings so much use direct language
Behaviors taught	how to be ladylike, polite, gentle how to rely on others, especially males, for help allowed to express emotions may learn they must rely on beauty more than intelligence to attract men	how to behave like men encouraged to be independent and strong and to avoid being "mama's boys" told that boys don't cry
Parent's social expectations	expected to think more about the family (e.g. remember birthdays) thought to need more protection	expected to be independent expected to be more interested in the world outside the family allowed more freedom

2 If your students are all from the same country, there will undoubtedly still be differences in the ways children are brought up in individual families. Encourage as much discussion as possible.

Task 2 LANGUAGE FOCUS: LINKING WORDS

1,2 Make sure students understand the meaning of the terms *comparison* (talking or writing about similarities) and *contrast* (talking or writing about differences). Becoming confident with linking words like those in the chart takes time and practice. It can be difficult to explain to students why one linking word or phrase is better than another. Encourage them to take notice of these expressions when reading and to write down and collect examples to guide them when writing.

3 Answers

  1 In contrast

  2 while *or* whereas

  3 and

  4 whereas

  5 Similarly *or* In the same way

  6 both...and

Task 3 WRITING A COMPARISON AND CONTRAST TEXT

Many students find writing comparison and contrast texts challenging. This is often because they do not plan the organization of the text well enough beforehand, and then get into difficulty when writing. The graphic illustration in the task commentary box will help them visualize the two common methods: linear and zigzag.

Discuss the advantages and disadvantages of both patterns and their usefulness in different writing contexts. For example, in a two- or three-page essay, the zigzag pattern is better because the reader can keep track more easily of the points of comparison or contrast. In a short essay, the linear method may be adequate.

1 | The purpose of this activity is to familiarize students with the two methods of organization. Students should find the actual task easy to do. Explain that more than one word may be required to complete each space.

Answers

From the moment of birth, babies are usually treated according to their gender. In the United States and in many other countries, baby girls tend to be dressed in pink clothing. They are <u>handled</u> gently, cuddled, and kissed a great deal and <u>given dolls</u> as toys. Mothers think a lot about how pretty their little girls should look. Baby boys, in contrast, are <u>dressed in blue</u>. They are not handled as gently as girls and are bounced around and <u>lifted high in the air</u>. Boys are given cars, trucks, and building blocks as toys. Another difference is that mothers are <u>less concerned about their little boys' appearance</u>.

2 | Elicit the idea that a chart would be a good way to take notes from the paragraph. You could ask students to do this after they have discussed the paragraph.

Answers

zigzag method

3 | Have students reread paragraph 5 of the text to stimulate their ideas on the kinds of things they might write about. If there are students from the same country in your class, you could put them together to discuss the topic before writing. Make sure students decide which method they are going to use before they start to write.

4 | You could suggest that partners take notes in chart form from each other's writing as a check on the clarity of their organizational method.

2 FAIRY-TALE LESSONS FOR GIRLS

Preparing to read (Student's Book pg. 60)

THINKING ABOUT THE TOPIC

1 | Encourage as much discussion as possible. Elicit examples of different fairy tales or children's stories.

2 | You might stimulate students to begin this task by retelling a fairy tale that you know.

BUILDING VOCABULARY: LEARNING WORDS RELATED TO THE TOPIC

Clarify meanings as needed. You might explain to students, for example, that in fairy tales, the *godmother* is usually a *fairy godmother*, that is, an imaginary creature that fulfills the role of a human godmother to watch over the welfare of a child.

Answers

People	Words to describe people	Nonhuman creatures	Places	Actions
heroine	brave	fairy	tower	slay
magician	handsome	beast	cottage	rescue
hero	wicked	dragon	forest	turn into
witch	evil	monster	castle	
godmother	cruel			
stepmother				
prince				
princess				

Now read

Refer to page xi of this Teacher's Manual for suggestions about ways in which students can read the text.

After you read (Student's Book pg. 63)

Task 1 WRITING SHORT ANSWERS TO TEST QUESTIONS

Read through the task commentary box with your students. Emphasize the frequency with which they will encounter this type of test question in colleges and universities, and how important it is that they master this method of responding.

1 | Give your students time to study the example. Elicit explanations of how the highlighted parts of the text are used in the answer.

2 Encourage students to use the linking words for comparison and contrast texts that were presented in Task 2, Language Focus: Linking Words, in Section 1, "After You Read" on page 57 of the Student's Book.

Sample answers

1 Women have usually been given the roles of wives, mothers, or imaginary creatures such as witches or fairy godmothers. In contrast, men have been given a larger range of roles, for example, fighters, policemen, judges, and kings.

2 Some people argue that these traditional stereotypes are damaging for little girls because they make them want to be beautiful rather than strong, powerful, and clever.

3 Some authors and filmmakers are creating heroines who are strong, brave, and clever.

Task 2 APPLYING WHAT YOU READ

1 Ask students to skim "Rapunzel" and look at the illustrations. Elicit language from students to describe the illustrations. Then allow time for students to read the story, or read through the story with them.

2 **Sample answers**
   - The wife is cast in a secondary role – weak and ill – while her husband is cast as the actor (he goes and gets the herbs).
   - Another major female role is an imaginary one, that is, a witch.
   - The bad woman, the witch, is ugly and cruel, while the good girl, Rapunzel, is beautiful.
   - Rapunzel is a passive character because she is dependent on the witch.
   - The handsome prince falls in love with the beautiful Rapunzel the first time he sees her.
   - The prince and Rapunzel marry and live happily ever after.

3 Encourage students to defend their opinions with examples from their own experience.

Task 3 WRITING A PERSUASIVE TEXT

Work through the writing steps and the model essay, "The Frog Prince," with your students. Explain that it is important to "say what the story is about," that is, to summarize, without getting too tied up in details. Students could practice summarizing the story orally either to you or to other students before they start to write. You may want to assign the actual writing as homework.

3 LEARNING GENDER LESSONS AT SCHOOL

Preparing to read (Student's Book pg. 66)

EXAMINING GRAPHIC MATERIAL

1,2 | **Answers**

    <u>T</u> **1**

    <u>F</u> **2**

    <u>T</u> **3**

3 | Encourage as much discussion as possible.

PREDICTING

1,2 | Remind students of the value of predicting when reading. Explain that it is not important that they get the right answers at this prereading stage. The point is that thinking about the topic prepares them for reading. After they have read the text, remind students to check their answers to the questions.

    Answers

    1 women

    2 men

    3 less

    4 more

Now read

Refer to page xi of this Teacher's Manual for suggestions about ways in which students can read the text.

After you read (Student's Book pg. 69)

Task 1 WRITING A ONE-SENTENCE SUMMARY

1 | Make sure that students understand they are looking for a sentence that captures the meaning of the whole text, not just one part.

    Answers

    b

2 | **Sample answer**

The text "Learning Gender Lessons at School" describes the ways schools give messages to boys and girls about gender roles and some recent concerns about boys. It describes, for example, how children may get the message that women need men to lead them because, at school, they see that most teachers are female but most principals are male. The text also discusses concerns about boys' behavior and academic performance compared to girls'.

3 | Draw students' attention to the usefulness of rereading introductory paragraphs and headings when summarizing a text. Tell students to keep their summaries written for this step and for step 2 for possible use in the Chapter Writing Assignment.

Sample answers

"Bringing Up Boys and Girls" discusses the way we learn our gender roles when we are growing up.

"Fairy-Tale Lessons for Girls" discusses the influence of traditional fairy tales on girls' thoughts and behavior.

Task 2 BUILDING VOCABULARY: USING CONTEXT CLUES

Answers

_g_ **1**

_e_ **2**

_a_ **3**

_b_ **4**

_d_ **5**

_f_ **6**

_h_ **7**

_c_ **8**

Task 3 PERSONAL WRITING

Explain to students that personal writing does not have to be structured in any particular way. Tell them to keep their personal writing for possible use in the Chapter Writing Assignment.

4 | GENDER ROLES IN THE MEDIA

Preparing to read (Student's Book pg. 70)

PREVIEWING ART IN THE TEXT

Point out to students that the cartoon both stereotypes male and female gender roles and makes fun of the stereotypes, if they do not make this observation in their discussions. You can also draw the students' attention to the second cartoon in the text (on page 72 of the Student's Book), and ask them to examine it in the same way.

SPEED-READING TECHNIQUES

Stress how important it is that students develop the habit of reading quickly when doing academic work. Be sure to read carefully each point in the task commentary box with your students.

Give students a time goal of about 4 minutes to read the text. This is not too fast and should be manageable for students using these techniques for the first time.

Tell students they only need to give brief and general answers to the six questions, which are included to show them that even when reading fast they can still understand considerable detail in a text.

Do not provide students with the correct answers at this point. Make sure, however, that you check their answers with them after a second, slower reading and before they do the "After You Read" tasks.

Answers

1 newspapers, magazines, TV commercials, TV programs, cartoons, film, comic strips

2 how to care for families, beauty advice

3 as sex objects and as housewives

4 that successful women should also be sexy

5 TV cartoons

6 The points from Spicher and Hudak's research are enumerated in the boxed text on page 72 of the Student's Book. Possible answers:

• that there had been little change in gender stereotyping in TV cartoons for young people since the 1970s

• that male cartoon characters on TV were more prominent than female characters

• that male characters had more interesting personalities than female characters

• that males were more powerful, strong, smart, and aggressive

• that female characters were colorless and boring

• that there were still only a small number of female characters shown in nontraditional occupations such as doctors or police officers

Now read

Refer to page xi of this Teacher's Manual for suggestions about ways in which students can read the text.

After students read the text this time, have them check their answers. Then review the answers with the class.

After you read (Student's Book pg. 73)

Task 1 READING FOR DETAIL

You might want to ask students to copy the chart headings on a separate piece of paper and fill in the answers there. This will encourage them to write as much as possible.

Sample answers

	In the past	Today
Women's magazines	Focused on caring for families and beauty advice	Many still define the female role in terms of homemaking and motherhood; some non-traditional magazines show women in a range of roles and have a wider range of topics; traditional magazines still dominate.
TV commercials	Women presented as sex objects or as housewives	Advertisers are more careful that women are presented in a variety of roles; it is still common to see advertisements where beautiful women are used to sell products.
Prime-time TV shows	Women shown as lovers, mothers, or weak, passive girlfriends of powerful, effective men	Women are shown as successful, and able to support themselves and their families; storylines suggest that to be successful women need to be sexy, too.
TV cartoons	Male characters outnumbered females; male characters had more interesting personalities than female characters; males were more powerful, strong, smart, and aggressive; female characters were colorless and boring; there were a small number of females in nontraditional occupations such as doctors or police officers.	There is little change.

Task 2 LANGUAGE FOCUS: THE PASSIVE VOICE

Make sure that students understand the reasons for using the passive voice. Explain that, in general, either the active or the passive voice will dominate in a text, depending on the type of text and the topic.

1 | Circulate among the pairs, helping as necessary. Then elicit some examples, write them on the board, and discuss.

2 | Emphasize that students should keep the meaning of the sentence exactly the same.

Sample answers

2 In advertisements these days, men are often shown doing the washing and cooking dinner.

3 More men than women are used to anchor news programs.

4 In the fifties, women on TV were cast only in roles as mothers and homemakers.

5 Increasingly, women in TV programs are shown in roles that have traditionally been men's.

6 Women are still often portrayed in stereotypical gender roles.

3 | It would be a good idea to have magazines on hand for students to look at, or to bring to class some examples of cartoons and advertisements. Encourage discussion of the cartoons or advertisements students have chosen before they begin writing.

Task 3 READING CRITICALLY

Discuss the importance of critical reading, particularly in academic contexts.

1 | Draw students' attention to the distinction between statements of opinion and factual evidence. In this text, students will find that paragraphs mostly contain statements of opinion with perhaps one example of research evidence to support the opinion. Opinions in academic textbooks are usually based on research evidence, but not all examples of the research may be mentioned. Encourage students to examine the text and find instances where they would like to see more research evidence to support the opinions given.

2 | In response to question 3, make sure that students support their opinions with references to the examples they gave for questions 1 and 2.

Chapter 3 WRITING ASSIGNMENT (Student's Book pg. 75)

Read through the assignment choices with your students, eliciting from them which texts might be helpful to review prior to writing about each one. The choices for this writing assignment vary in difficulty regarding content and organization; therefore, you might wish to make suggestions to individual students about which ones they choose. You may want to put students who are going to write about the same topic in pairs or small groups to brainstorm ideas before they write and to give each other feedback afterwards.

Refer to the discussion of the Chapter 1 Writing Assignment on page 11 of this Teacher's Manual for further suggestions.

Chapter 4

Gender issues today

1 BALANCING HOME AND WORK

Preparing to read (Student's Book pg. 76)

THINKING ABOUT THE TOPIC

1 | Be sure to elicit ideas about the particular focus of each article as well as about the overall theme.

2 | Encourage discussion of both what students think should happen and what they think actually does happen. Explore any differences related to cultural backgrounds if they arise.

Now read

Refer to page xi of this Teacher's Manual for suggestions about ways in which students can read the text.

After you read (Student's Book pg. 80)

Task 1 READING FOR DETAIL

1 | **Answers**

  1 b

  2 Women do approximately twice as much housework as men do.

3 So far, no government anywhere has taken action to pay people to do housework. It would be very difficult to implement such a scheme. Some problems would be determining the amount to be paid, which tasks would be paid, whether different amounts would be paid to different people, and how to know if the tasks were done.

4 Disadvantages:
- may have role overload
- may have negative self-concept
- can lack self-confidence
- can find it difficult to develop new activities and interests when children leave home

Advantages:
- live longer
- can express emotions easily
- have closer bond with children
- are not only identified by their employment
- have many options

5 They agree to do something but then ask directions all the time. They argue that children should do the job. They go so slowly that their wives won't ask them to help again. They do the chores, but complain about it and make their wives upset and angry.

Task 2 LANGUAGE FOCUS: FIGURES OF SPEECH

Explain to students that the meaning of figures of speech can often be guessed from the literal meaning. After they do the sentence-completion exercise, ask for volunteers to explain the relationship between the literal and the figurative meaning of each item.

Answers
1 iron out

2 stretched

3 want it both ways

4 shoulder the main burden

5 the lion's share

Task 3 PERSONALIZING THE TOPIC

1 | Make sure students understand the meaning of each household chore, asking for volunteers to explain terms if needed.

2 | Encourage as much discussion as possible, especially for question 5. Elicit examples where appropriate. Refer back to the discussion of the four different family situations in step 2 of "Thinking About the Topic" on page 76 of the Student's Book.

Before students begin writing, elicit suggestions about how they might organize their ideas, for example, by following the five questions in step 2. Students should be encouraged to include information about how individuals in the group agreed or differed in their opinions or about particularly interesting or unusual views.

2 IT'S NOT SO EASY BEING MALE

Preparing to read (Student's Book pg. 82)

PREVIEWING TEXT HEADINGS

Stress that looking at headings is a key aspect of skimming and gives clues to both the content and organization of the text.

1 Explain to the students that it does not matter if their ideas are exactly right. The purpose of the exercise is to get them thinking of possibilities.

2 Make sure that students do this step without looking at the text.

Answers

<u>2</u> **a**

<u>4</u> **b**

<u>5</u> **c**

<u>1</u> **d**

<u>3</u> **e**

3 Get students to scan as quickly as they can, looking only to confirm their answers. Make sure they check their answers again after reading the text, and before they do the "After You Read" tasks.

Now read

Refer to page xi of this Teacher's Manual for suggestions about ways in which students can read the text.

After reading the text, give students time to check their answers to step 2 in "Previewing Text Headings" on page 82 of the Student's Book. Review the answers with the class.

After you read (Student's Book pg. 85)

Task 1 UNDERSTANDING PRONOUN REFERENCE

Stress the importance of being able to follow pronoun reference in comprehending whole texts, especially academic texts.

Answers

1 that the man pays the bills

2 Some men have never learned to cook, wash clothes, or take care of a home.

3 getting caught up in the job and not allowing enough time for family

4 "new age" men

Task 2 APPLYING WHAT YOU READ

1,2 This article refers to some extent to all the issues mentioned in the text. Encourage reference to these issues in the class discussion. If it arises, encourage discussion of how Stan's actions would be viewed in different cultures. Ask students what they think about Stan's decision. Ask them if they know any men who have done what Stan has done.

Task 3 PERSONAL WRITING

Remind students to focus on writing down their ideas more than on grammatical correctness.

③ INEQUALITY AT WORK

Preparing to read (Student's Book pg. 86)

THE SQR3 SYSTEM (PART I)

Have your students read the task commentary box. Explain that they have been putting the SQR3 approach into practice in many of the "Preparing to Read" tasks they have done so far.

1-3 Read through each of the explanations and instructions for these first three steps with your students. Be sure that students have time to survey the text, as instructed in step 1, and question the text, as instructed in step 2.

Now read

Refer to page xi of this Teacher's Manual for suggestions about ways in which students can read the text.

After you read (Student's Book pg. 89)

Task 1 THE SQR3 SYSTEM (PART II)

1 Emphasize how telling someone else about a text you have read helps you to understand and remember it. Remind students to include information about a graph if there is one in the paragraph they are telling a partner about. Encourage students to ask each other questions if they don't understand what their partner means.

2 | To save time in class, you might want to assign this step for homework. If you do, be sure to allow time in the next class for students to discuss in small groups any parts of the text they didn't understand. Circulate among the groups to clarify points as necessary.

Task 2 BUILDING VOCABULARY: COLLOCATIONS

Answers
- to deny <u>the right</u>
- to pass <u>a law</u>
- to take <u>a job</u>
- to enter <u>an occupation</u>
- to hold <u>a job</u>
- to solve <u>a problem</u>
- to fight for <u>a right</u>
- to pursue <u>a career</u>
- to follow <u>a lead</u>

You may want to extend this activity by asking students for other verbs that go with the nouns above (for example: *face* a problem, *have* a problem, *overcome* a problem) or other nouns that go with the verbs (for example: fight for *justice*, fight for *equality*).

Task 3 SUMMARIZING
Remind students to pay attention to the introduction, headings, and first sentences when writing summaries.

Sample answer
The text "Inequality at Work" discusses the problems women face in the workplace because of sexism. Although women have achieved equality in many areas, inequality in the workplace still exists. Women still generally work in lower-status, lower-paying jobs and in traditional female occupations. One reason for this, according to Schwartz (1989), is that many women are "career-and-family" women rather than "career-primary" women. They want to work, but they also want to participate fully in raising their children. To do this, they are willing to take jobs with lower pay because they can quit them at any time to take care of their families. Although there are more women in jobs traditionally held by men these days, they still tend to earn less then men.

4 SEXUAL HARASSMENT

Preparing to read (Student's Book pg. 90)

EXAMINING GRAPHIC MATERIAL

1 | **Answers**
Table 4.2 answers the question "How often does sexual harassment occur?"
Table 4.3 answers the question "What is sexual harassment?"

2 | Be sure students understand the vocabulary in the tables before the
paired discussions.

THINKING ABOUT THE TOPIC

1,2 | Give students time to read all the remarks. Then have pairs of students act out the
situations, with male students being the boss and female students being the
worker. Encourage a lighthearted approach. You could discuss how different
emphasis and intonation might affect the way in which the comments are
interpreted. Also ask students to consider other factors that might affect how they
view the comments.

After students have recorded their individual answers in the chart and compared
them in groups, ask them if their responses would be different if similar
comments were made by a female boss to a male worker.

Now read

Refer to page xi of this Teacher's Manual for suggestions about ways in which students
can read the text.

After you read (Student's Book pg. 94)

Task 1 SCANNING

Remind students to scan quickly for the answers. You might want to set a time limit.

Answers

1 unwanted sexual advances

2 Barbara Gutek

3 9.6% of women and 1.2% of men

4 what happens when expectations about behavior are carried over from other domains
(for example, the home) into the workplace

5 85.5% of women and 70.3% of men

6 Can I compliment a co-worker about his or her appearance? *or* Can I ask a co-worker
out on a date? *or* Should I avoid being alone with another worker?

Task 2 LANGUAGE FOCUS: EXPRESSING NUMERICAL DATA

Read through the task commentary box and the chart in step 1 with students.

2 | This task would make a good homework assignment, if you want to save time in class. You might encourage students to write more than five sentences, given the variety of possibilities in the text.

Task 3 READING CRITICALLY

Read through the task commentary box with your students and discuss any questions.

1 | **Answers**

1 We know how many people were surveyed (1,232 women and men); we know where the survey was done (in Los Angeles County) and we know that the results were published in 1985.

2 We might like to know:
- how old the subjects were

- how the subjects were chosen

- how the subjects were surveyed: face to face? by phone? in groups or individually?; if in groups, were the groups of mixed gender or segregated?

- what sort of workplace the subjects worked in

All the factors above may have affected the answers given by the subjects.

2 | Encourage students to use different texts so that you can get a variety of responses.

Task 4 THINKING ABOUT THE TOPIC

Keep in mind that sexual harassment is a sensitive issue and that there is likely to be a diversity of views on these questions.

Chapter 4 WRITING ASSIGNMENT (Student's Book pg. 96)

Read through the topics with students, eliciting from them which texts might be helpful to review prior to writing about each topic. You may want to put students who are going to write about the same topic in pairs or small groups to brainstorm ideas before they write and to give each other feedback afterwards.

Refer to the discussion of the Chapter 1 Writing Assignment on page 11 of this Teacher's Manual for further suggestions.

Media and Society

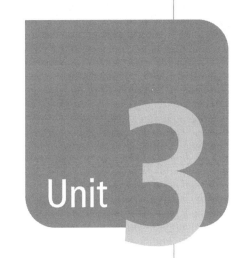

Unit title page (Student's Book pg. 97)

Ask students to explain the words in the title. (For *media* students may give examples of different kinds of media.) Ask students to look at the picture to suggest ways that the two concepts – *media* and *society* – might be connected. Read the unit summary paragraph to preview the content of the unit.

Previewing the unit (Student's Book pg. 98)

Chapter 5: Mass Media Today

1 Elicit some definitions of mass media and write them on the board. Explain that the word *media* is the plural of *medium* and that it is used interchangeably with *channel* when we refer to a *medium* (or *channel*) *of communication*. Although grammatically speaking the word *media* is a plural form, it is often used as a singular word (followed by a singular verb form), meaning all parts of the media industry taken as a whole.

2 Write a list of students' answers on the board. Ask students in which language they access which media, and why.

3 Have students read the first paragraph of the article on page 101 to check answers to steps 1 and 2.

Chapter 6: The Influence of the Media

Make sure students understand the title of Chapter 6.

1 Have students discuss the meanings in groups and then check them in a dictionary.

Sample answers
censorship: controls imposed by governments or the media industry itself on what can be published or broadcast. Violence, pornography, or certain political stories may be censored in some countries.
privacy: Sometimes the media publishes details of the private lives of famous people, or films people with a hidden camera, which may deny their rights to privacy.
truth: The public expects the media to tell the truth. However, news reporting is done by individuals with particular views of the world; therefore, it always involves some opinion, and sometimes the facts are distorted.
propaganda: We usually think of propaganda in a political sense, where one political group uses the media to persuade people to believe certain things and to not believe other things. But whenever the media is used to convert us to a point of view, we could call this propaganda. Thus, propaganda is also part of advertising.

2 Have one member of each group report to the class what his or her group discussed.

Chapter 5

Mass Media Today

1 THE ROLE OF MASS MEDIA

Preparing to read (Student's Book pg. 100)

PERSONALIZING THE TOPIC

Ask students to compare their information in small groups. You could also elicit from the class, by a show of hands, the time spent using different media, and record numbers of students on a chart like the one below.

MEDIA	0–5 hrs/wk	6–10 hrs/wk	11–15 hrs/wk	16–20 hrs/wk	20+ hrs/wk
TV					
Internet					

BUILDING VOCABULARY: LEARNING WORDS RELATED TO THE TOPIC

1, 2 | If possible, students should describe the program type in general terms as well as providing a specific example and a likely time for broadcast. Access to a local TV guide will help.

Answers
- talk shows: programs where one or more guests (famous or otherwise) are invited to talk to a host. There is usually a live studio audience.

- news: usually 30 or 60 minutes in length; may contain both local and international news; usually shown at about 6:00 or 7:00 A.M., 6:00 or 7:00 P.M., and 10:00 or 11:00 P.M.

- prime-time movies: movies shown at the time most people are watching TV, that is in midevening.

- late-night talk shows: similar to daytime talk shows, but the guests are usually famous people, and there are also other kinds of entertainment, such as music. As the name suggests, the shows are usually broadcast in the late evening, perhaps 10:00 or 11:00 P.M.

- soap operas: dramas or comedies where one episode (usually 30 or 60 minutes long) of an ongoing story is broadcast daily or once a week; in the day or evening.

- cartoons: animated drawings that are usually humorous, often intended for children.

- comedies: any program designed to make people laugh; usually shown in midevening.

- documentaries: factual programs that report on people, places, or things; often shown in the evening or on weekends.

3 | Have students compare their answers in pairs.

Now read

Refer to page xi of this Teacher's Manual for suggestions about ways in which students can read the text.

After you read (Student's Book pg. 104)

Task 1 LINKING IDEAS IN A TEXT

1 | **Answer**
The word *includes* signals that a list will follow. It appears in the second sentence of paragraph 1, which begins, "Mass media includes . . . ."

2 | **Answers**

Par.	Functions of the media	Linking expressions
3	entertainment	none
4	education	Another . . .
5	warnings	none
6	shaping beliefs and opinions	In addition . . .
7	socialization; companionship	A further . . . ; Finally, . . .

3 | **Sample answer**
The media fulfills many functions in our daily lives. These include education, or learning about the world, and socialization, or learning how to behave in a certain culture. There are <u>other</u> functions <u>too</u>, such as giving warnings of potential danger as well as shaping the beliefs and values of the viewer. <u>And finally</u>, the media can provide people with entertainment and companionship.

Task 2 APPLYING WHAT YOU READ

1 | Direct students to read the boxed text at the end of the reading passage on page 103. Then refer them back to their answers in step 2 of "Personalizing the Topic" on page 100.

Provide examples of a local weekday TV viewing guide, or ask students to bring copies in to class, so that there is at least one guide per group of students. Have each group compare their findings with another group.

3 | **Sample answers**
Cartoons are likely to be broadcast in the early morning and in the time after school, when many parents allow (or even encourage) their children to watch TV.

Programs targeted to female viewers, such as some soap operas, are shown during the day, when it is assumed more women will be at home looking after children. The news is broadcast to coincide with the time before many people go to work, the time when many people return home from work, and the time when people have completed their evening activities and are preparing for bed. Movies are shown in mid- to late evening when people have eaten their evening meal and have time to relax.

Task 3 HIGHLIGHTING

Ask if students use this strategy when reading and how useful they find it. Explain that in order for highlighting to be useful, only key words and phrases should be highlighted. Emphasize the importance of reviewing highlighted text to retain an understanding of it.

1 | **Sample answer**
The mass media is an important part of life in the United States and most Americans are exposed to the media daily in the form of print, sound waves, and pictures. Over 55 million newspapers are circulated each day. There are over five radios per household , and it is estimated that radio reaches 77 percent of people over the age of 12 every day . The radio listening time for those over 12 is more than three hours each day . Most households also have two or more television sets , with a total viewing time of about seven hours per day . The amount of time that people spend in front of their television sets varies with age, gender, and education, but on average it amounts to three to four hours a day .

2 | Review with students some note-taking signs and abbreviations that will be helpful for this task, for example:

more than = >

over 12 = 12+

percent = %

million = m

per = /

Answers

Form of media	Facts and Figures
1) Newspapers	>55m/day
2) Radios	>5 per household; 77% of 12+ listen for 3+ hrs/day
3) TV	2 or more sets/household; 7 hrs/day; avg. 3–4hrs/day

2 WHAT IS NEWSWORTHY?

Preparing to read (Student's Book pg. 106)

THINKING ABOUT THE TOPIC

1,2 | Have students do these steps individually and then compare their answers with a group. Elicit from each group the factors that they think make a story newsworthy and write them on the board. Keep the list to refer back to after the next task.

SKIMMING

1 | Tell students they have a time limit of 30 seconds to skim the text for the words in italics. Elicit the words they recorded and write them on the board. All of these words are terms related to what makes a story newsworthy.

2 | Give students 1 minute to skim the text again for information to explain the terms. Discuss the meaning of the terms as a class. Then compare the factors with the list of factors the students compiled in the previous task.

Now read

Refer to page xi of this Teacher's Manual for suggestions about ways in which students can read the text.

After you read (Student's Book pg. 109)

Task 1 APPLYING WHAT YOU READ

1 | Have students quickly review and list the newsworthiness factors in the text.

2 | **Sample answers**
These are sample answers from the point of view of someone living in San Francisco. Note that timeliness is an assumed factor for all of these headlines.
   1 negative

   2 geographic proximity; famous city; unexpected; facts and figures

   3 negative; geographic proximity

   4 unexpected; facts and figures; clear and unambiguous

    5 negative; unexpected; facts and figures

    6 negative; famous person

    7 unexpected; facts and figures; assumed geographic proximity

3 | This task could be done as a homework assignment. Students can then report to the class.

Task 2 READING NEWS STORIES

Explain that the main facts (and figures, if any) in a news story are presented in the opening sentence so that the reader can find out about the event as quickly as possible. The rest of the news story gives more information and explanation.

1 | **Sample answers**

Story 1: What happened? Where did it happen? When did it happen? How much snow fell? How many flights were canceled?

Story 2: Who won? What did he/she win? Where was it? How many races did he/she win?

2 | Tell students that before writing, they should make a list of "Why" and "How" questions and then make notes about what the answers will be. Explain that which facts they put first will give the story a particular angle or emphasis.

Sample answers
- Two bank robbers (*who*) were arrested (*what*) last night (*when*) as they tried to escape (*when*) after stealing $500,000 (*how much*) from the Denver branch of the Colorado State Bank (*where*).

- A daring raid on the Denver branch of the Colorado State Bank last night, in which thieves stole $500,000, ended in the arrest of two men.

3 REPORTING THE FACTS

Preparing to read (Student's Book pg. 110)

REVIEWING PREVIOUS READINGS

Ask one or two students to summarize the main points of the commentary box for the class.

BUILDING VOCABULARY: PREFIXES

Read through the task commentary box. Elicit several more examples to check students' understanding of prefixes and suffixes.

1 | **Answers**
- *misreports*: reports inaccurately
- *misheard*: heard incorrectly

- *misquoted*: quoted inaccurately

"Mis" adds the meaning of *wrongly* or *inaccurately* to the original word.

2 | Answers
- "centi" = one hundred

  A *centimeter* is one hundredth of a meter.

  Sample answers

  centigrade; *century*
- "re" = again

  Rearranging means arranging again (arranging in a different way).

  Sample answers

  reproduce; *reapply*
- "un" = not

  Unverified means not checked for the truth.

  Sample answers

  uninteresting; *unbelievable*

Now read

Refer to page xi of this Teacher's Manual for suggestions about ways in which students can read the text.

After you read (Student's Book pg. 113)

Task 1 SCANNING

Remind students to scan quickly for the answers. You might want to set a time limit.

1 | Answers

1 b

2 c

3 d

4 a

2 | Answers

1 one to two centimeters a year, not eight

2 "That was the one . . . ", not "I was the one . . . "

3 There were no riots.

4 Bob Hope was not dead.

3 | Discuss this with the whole class.

Task 2 ASKING FOR CLARIFICATION

Read through the task commentary box with students. Some of them may not be used to asking questions in class or participating in discussion. Be sure they understand that participation is expected and encouraged in most college and university classrooms in English-speaking countries.

Ask students to find the relevant paragraph, discuss the meanings of the phrases/clauses in question, and then practice asking and responding to the requests for clarification.

3 You could offer some further examples, such as, "I'm not sure what the author means when he says that rumors spread 'by word of mouth'?" (par. 7)

Task 3 BUILDING VOCABULARY: COLLOCATIONS

1,2 Answers
The collocations used in the text are shown with *.

common	false	enormous	deliberate	serious	exact
criticism	information*	criticism*	strategy*	criticism	information
complaint*		impact		complaint	words*
words				impact*	
strategy				words	

3 Answers
- to publish false information / the exact words
- to have a serious impact / an enormous impact / a deliberate strategy
- to make a serious complaint / an enormous criticism / a serious criticism
- to plan a deliberate strategy
- to record a common complaint / a serious criticism / the exact words / the exact information
- to give false information / serious criticism / the exact words / the exact information

Task 4 SUMMARIZING

Answers
News reports in the media sometimes contain information that is not <u>accurate</u>. This may result from simple slips or insufficient checking of <u>facts</u>, or it may be the result of deliberate <u>exaggeration</u> to make the story more <u>newsworthy</u>. People are sometimes <u>misquoted</u>, that is, they are reported as using words they did not use, or they are reported as giving answers to <u>questions</u> that they were not actually asked. Sometimes people are reported as saying something when they have never even spoken to <u>reporters</u>. The Internet is not always reliable. It is a source of <u>rumors</u>, where unchecked facts are picked up and circulated widely around the world.

4 ADVERTISING IN THE MEDIA

Preparing to read (Student's Book pg. 116)

THINKING ABOUT THE TOPIC

1 | Elicit answers from the class as a whole. Most of the advertisements that students mention are likely to come from TV. If that is so, discuss why. It may be the use of catchy jingles, moving visual images, or the frequency with which the advertisements are broadcast.

2 | If students are from different countries and cultures, discuss and compare advertising practices and rules in those countries.

READING AROUND THE TOPIC

Answers

1 A "blink ad" is the length of a blink of an eye. If we blink, we might miss it.

2 A snack is something quick and light to eat, usually between meals. One-second ads are "snack-proof" because they do not allow time to go to the kitchen for a snack and, thus, miss the advertisement. Many people like to use the remote control to "zap" (that is, to change) TV channels when the ad breaks are on. The ads are "zap-proof" because they do not allow time to do this.

3 The symbols or logos would have to be very well known so that they could be recognized in one second, for example, logos of McDonalds, Coca-Cola, or Nike.

Now read

Refer to page xi of this Teacher's Manual for suggestions about ways in which students can read the text.

After you read (Student's Book pg. 120)

Task 1 APPLYING WHAT YOU READ

1 | **Sample answers**
   - Tropical island holiday
     strategy: creates image of idyllic location
     target audience: working people who want a relaxing vacation
   - Shampoo
     strategies: eye contact; close-up photo of model
     target audience: men who want to be attractive to women
   - Toyota
     strategy: alliteration
     target audience: people who feel (or want to feel) that they are up-to-date and aware of the latest ideas

- Milk
  strategies: famous people; eye contact; cultural references
  target audience: young people who identify with the success and physical fitness of Venus and Serena Williams.

2 | Answers will vary from individual to individual as well as from culture to culture, although there is likely to be agreement about some colors. Ask students to consider what colors they would or would not choose for an advertisement for a bathroom cleaner or for a luxury car, and why. Have students suggest other colors and associations.

3 | This task can be undertaken as a group project. Groups can report back to the class on their findings.

Task 2 BUILDING VOCABULARY: DEALING WITH UNKNOWN WORDS

1 | **Answers**
- finding a definition within the text

- looking at the surrounding language for clues to meaning

- using knowledge of related words

- recognizing the part of speech of the word

2 | **Answers**
- glossy: shiny. A glossy magazine has high-quality, shiny paper.

- brand name: the manufacturer's name

- logo: the symbol of a company

- idyllic: pleasing or picturesque

- glamorous: appearance of wealth and beauty

- sequential: occurring one after the other

Task 3 DRAMATIZING THE TEXT

1-3 | The planning stages can be done in class, and the design and rehearsal stages can be done as out-of-class activities. Suggest that students watch some advertisements on TV to get ideas.

4 | Groups can rate each other on the performances and perhaps give a "Best TV Commercial" award to the winner.

Chapter 5 WRITING ASSIGNMENT (Student's Book pg. 121)

Read through the topics with your students, eliciting from them which texts might be helpful to review prior to writing about each topic. You may want to put students who are going to write about the same topic in pairs or small groups to brainstorm ideas before they write and to give each other feedback afterwards.

Refer to the discussion of the Chapter 1 Writing Assignment on page 11 of this Teacher's Manual for further suggestions.

Chapter 6

The Influence of the Media

1 PRIVACY AND THE MEDIA

Preparing to read (Student's Book pg. 122)

PREDICTING

1 | Elicit the names of the people in the photos (former U.S. President Bill Clinton and the late Diana, Princess of Wales), and find out what the students know about them.

2 | Write a few key words on the board based on the students' suggestions, but do not confirm answers. Tell students they will find answers when they read the text.

Answer
Bill Clinton and Princess Diana are public figures who both received a great deal of media attention in relation to their personal lives. The two examples mentioned in the text are Bill Clinton's relationship with Monica Lewinsky and Princess Diana's death in a car crash after the car had been chased by paparazzi.

THINKING ABOUT THE TOPIC

Begin by explaining that the role of the editorial board of a newspaper is to decide such things as which news stories to print, which stories to put on the front page, and what photographs to include. Students should try to reach a decision for each photograph within a time limit (for example, 2 minutes per photograph).

Sample answers
• Factors in favor of publication might include the following: sensational photographs sell more papers; the public has a right to know what is happening; a lack of privacy is the price of fame.

- Factors against publication might include the following: the stories represented in the photos are not important news stories; people have a right to privacy; people's lives may be adversely affected by the publication of the photo.

Now read

Refer to page xi of this Teacher's Manual for suggestions about ways in which students can read the text.

After you read (Student's Book pg. 126)

Task 1 READING FOR MAIN IDEAS

1 | **Answers**

  <u>4</u> **a**

  <u>2</u> **b**

  <u>1</u> **c**

  <u>6</u> **d**

  <u>3</u> **e**

  <u>5</u> **f**

2 | If students are unable to think of specific examples, they can discuss the kind of information about people's private lives that might damage their careers if it were publicized in the media.

  Sample answers
  A person has a particular illness or disease, a drinking or drug problem, marital or family problems, or a criminal record.

Task 2 BUILDING VOCABULARY: GUESSING THE MEANING FROM CONTEXT

Answers

<u>g</u> **1** drop out

<u>c</u> **2** dominated

<u>e</u> **3** scandal

<u>b</u> **4** aggressive

<u>f</u> **5** deliberately

<u>a</u> **6** embarrassing

<u>d</u> **7** unwelcome

<u>i</u> **8** investigate

<u>h</u> **9** coverage

Task 3 WRITING A DISCUSSION PARAGRAPH

1 | Check answers from one or two pairs of students. Discuss the fact that by putting one argument last in a discussion we can give the impression that we are more in favor of that argument. Illustrate this by changing the order of the two points of view in the paragraph and reading the new arrangement out loud to students.

Answer

A basic question for the media is <u>whether a politician's personal life is relevant to his or her performance in the job</u>. One point of view suggests that if a person is not honest and faithful to his or her spouse, that person will not be honest and faithful to his or her country . Another view says that if you get rid of everyone who has broken a moral law, there will be no one left to serve in public office .

2 | **Sample answers**

In favor: People have a right to know what is happening in their community.
Against: This would show a lack of respect for people's right to privacy.

3 | Remind students to use the structure for writing a discussion paragraph given in this task's commentary box, and to put last the argument(s) they favor.

2 INTERNET ISSUES

Preparing to read (Student's Book pg. 128)

READING AROUND THE TOPIC

Check what students already know about the Internet before they read the passage. Then ask them to read to find or confirm answers. Students can then ask and answer the questions with a partner to check their own understanding.

PERSONALIZING THE TOPIC

Have several students report what they discussed with their partners to the class. Others can say if their experience is similar or different. You could also discuss where students use the Internet (for example, at school or college, at home, at a public library, in an Internet café) and how the Internet might be used differently by different groups in society, such as the elderly, people in isolated communities, the police, or teachers.

SPEED READING

Review with the class the notes on speed-reading techniques in Chapter 3 on page 70 of the Student's Book. Explain that they should aim to finish the reading within 4 minutes. Tell them when the time is up, but allow all students to finish reading the passage. Explain that their reading will become faster the more they practice speed-reading techniques.

Now read

Refer to page xi of this Teacher's Manual for suggestions about ways in which students can read the text.

After reading the text, students should discuss with their partner from the speed-reading activity they did prior to this reading (on page 128 of the Student's Book) whether or not they still think the main ideas they discussed then represent the main ideas of the text.

After you read (Student's Book pg. 132)

Task 1 READING FOR MAIN IDEAS

1 | Have students do this task one paragraph at a time. Check answers after each paragraph.

Answers

par. 1: positive uses people make of the Internet

par. 2: concerns about the lack of controls on what people can access on the Internet

par. 3: concerns about a lack of privacy or security in Internet communications

par. 4: the misuse of the Internet in the workplace

par. 5: the problem of Internet addiction

2 | Elicit several topic sentences and write them on the board. Then have students discuss which sentence they prefer and why. Discuss whether students consider themselves or anyone they know to be an Internet addict. If so, what symptoms do they show?

Sample answers

• The following strategies may help you to avoid Internet addiction.

• There are a number of things you can do to overcome an Internet addiction.

Task 2 APPLYING WHAT YOU READ

Make sure students understand each item. Review the rating scale and explain that they should rate each statement by recording the relevant number. Remind them that the test applies only to nonwork or nonstudy purposes. When students have completed the test and added their scores, have them compare scores with several other students.

Elicit views on whether students think the results would give a good indication of levels of addiction. If not, have them suggest improvements to the existing test questions or come up with additional questions.

Elicit some additional advice to add to the list in step 2 of Task 1.

Task 3 THINKING ABOUT THE TOPIC

Begin by asking for views on whether there should be controls of the Internet with a show of hands. You could then group students into those who favor controls and those who oppose them. Each group records the arguments for their position. They then think of arguments that are likely to be made by the other group, and discuss how they could argue against those points. Have each group choose two or three spokespeople. Ask one spokesperson from each group in turn to present an argument. Each new speaker should try to respond to the previous speaker as well as to make his or her own point. Alternatively, you could follow up the discussion by asking students to write a discussion paragraph, reinforcing what they learned in the previous section, in Task 3, "Writing a Discussion Paragraph," on page 127.

3 PROPAGANDA AND THE MEDIA

Preparing to read (Student's Book pg. 134)

THINKING ABOUT THE TOPIC

1 | **Answers**

   c   **1**

   d   **2**

   b   **3**

   a   **4**

2 | Encourage students to note any contrasting words or expressions in each pair of headlines that signal different points of view. They should also note how different information is given more or less emphasis in one or the other headline.

   Sample answers
   1 *Peaceful* contrasts with *disrupt*. *Restore order* implies that there was disorder at some point.

   2 *Only military targets* contrasts with *women and children*.

   3 One headline emphasizes the reply to the criticism but the other emphasizes the criticism.

   4 One headline emphasizes the problem – *unemployment rising*. The other emphasizes the solution – *new plans*.

3 | Have students read out definitions they have found in the dictionary. Discuss examples of propaganda that they are aware of.

SKIMMING

1 | Give a time limit of 1 minute for students to look at headings and words in bold or italics in the text.

2 | **Answers**
   • "Why doesn't propaganda always work?"
   "We do not rely on just one source of ideas. There are many different influences on our thinking."

- "How does propaganda work?"
"By using language or visual images that encourage us to think positively or negatively about an idea"
- "What is propaganda?"
"Communication that is intended to shape our views or change our opinions"

Now read

Refer to page xi of this Teacher's Manual for suggestions about ways in which students can read the text.

After you read (Student's Book pg. 137)

Task 1 READING FOR THE MAIN IDEA

1 | **Answer**
c

2 | **Answers**
a Paragraphs 4 and 5

b Paragraph 1

d Paragraph 6

Task 2 BUILDING VOCABULARY: COLLOCATIONS

1,2 | **Answers**
The collocations used in the text are shown with *.
1 to win* our hearts and minds

2 to create* / to make a good impression

3 to make* / to create a profit

4 to gain* / to win mass support

5 to manipulate* / to shape public opinion

6 to shape* our views

Task 3 APPLYING WHAT YOU READ

Ask students to bring to class photographs from news stories or advertisements that they consider to be propaganda. Then have them discuss the photographs with a partner before they write. You might assign writing the paragraph for homework.

4 TELEVISION AND CHILDREN

Preparing to read (Student's Book pg. 138)

READING AROUND THE TOPIC

1,2 | Have students read the first short text quickly to identify the social problem(s) discussed, then report to their partner. Do the same for the remaining two short texts. Then have students discuss the impact of television on their own lives. Quickly survey the class (by a show of hands) on whether TV has generally had a positive or negative effect on their lives.

Answers to question 1 of step 2
- the problems of addiction
- poor eating habits, that is, the consumption of junk food
- violence is shown as glamorous or as entertainment

PREDICTING

1,2 | Give students time to brainstorm their lists. Then make a class list on the board. Have students discuss with their partners what topics and ideas they expect to find in the text. Circulate among the pairs, encouraging them to use words from the list on the board in discussing their predictions.

Now read

Refer to page xi of this Teacher's Manual for suggestions about ways in which students can read the text.

After you read (Student's Book pg. 141)

Task 1 TEST TAKING: ANSWERING TRUE/FALSE QUESTIONS

Before students read the information in the task commentary box, ask for a volunteer to explain what a true/false test is. Then ask members of the class if they have any advice they would give other students preparing to take a true/false test. Finally, have them read the box to see what advice is given.

Answers

F __ 1

T __ 2

F __ 3

F __ 4

T __ 5

T __ 6

F __ 7

Task 2 READING CRITICALLY

Read through the task commentary box with students. Ensure that they understand the difference between a causal relationship and a correlation.

1 | Review the first two examples with the students.

Answers

3 CO

4 CE

5 CE

6 CO

7 CE

8 CE

9 CE

2 | Monitor the task by moving around the class and helping the students with any statements they are having difficulty with. Review the answers with the whole class.

Task 3 LANGUAGE FOCUS: REPORTING VERBS

1 | **Answers**

2 –

3 –

4 +

5 +

2 | Have students read to the class two versions of the same statement using different reporting verbs to check if they have changed the degree of certainty.

Sample answers

2 pointed out

3 found

4 claimed

5 suggested

Task 4 CITING STUDIES IN YOUR WRITING

After reading through the task commentary box with your students, you might want to discuss citation forms required in college and university classes. Explain that there are variations in citation form and students should clarify with each professor which form he or she requires. You can also explain that there are writing handbooks available in most college bookstores that explain citation forms in more detail.

1 | Have students highlight places in the text where research findings are cited.

- The Henry J. Kaiser Family Foundation (1999) found that two-thirds of children 8 years or older have a TV set in their bedroom.
- A study of 1,600 television programs found that 80 percent contained violence (Matthews and Ellis 1985).
- By watching violence we become more sensitive to it (Tan 1985).
- Giddens (1991) suggests that we also need to consider the way the violence is presented and dealt with.
- Sixty percent of parents surveyed believed that television promotes violent behavior (Marklein 1989).

Chapter 6 WRITING ASSIGNMENT (Student's Book pg. 144)

Read through the topics with your students, eliciting from them which texts might be helpful to review prior to writing about each topic. You may want to put students who are going to write about the same topic in pairs or small groups to brainstorm ideas before they write and to give each other feedback afterwards.

Refer to the discussion of the Chapter 1 Writing Assignment on page 11 of this Teacher's Manual for further suggestions.

Breaking the Rules

Unit title page (Student's Book pg. 145)

As a class, have students brainstorm any words or expressions related to crime, while you record them on the board. Then ask students to read the unit introduction and highlight the words that indicate the content of each chapter. (Chapter 7: "kinds of crime and criminals; solving crime with . . . developments in science and technology." Chapter 8: "ways of preventing or controlling crime; different means of punishing criminals; the death penalty.") Have students use these words as category headings. Under these headings they can try to group as many words as possible from the list that they brainstormed.

Previewing the unit (Student's Book pg. 146)

Chapter 7: Crime and Criminals

1 Ask one student to suggest the correct statement for each point. Have the rest of the class indicate with a show of hands if they agree. Do not say if they are correct or not. Students can check their predictions after they have completed sections 1 and 2 of Chapter 7.

Answers

1 More	**4** most
2 less	**5** people known to the victim
3 more	**6** weekends

2 First draw students' attention to the photograph, and discuss what it shows. You may need to provide the term *magnifying glass*. There is no one right answer here, and students should return to this question after they have read sections 3 and 4 of Chapter 7.

Chapter 8: Controlling Crime

1 As an aid to doing this task, suggest that students refer back to the list they brainstormed during the discussion of the opening page of this unit (page 145 of the Student's Book). Record responses on the board in two columns – "punishments" and "crimes." If there is disagreement about how particular crimes should be punished, encourage students to justify their views.

2 Call on several groups to give a summary of their discussions for the rest of the class.

Chapter 7

Crime and criminals

1 DEVIANCE AND CRIME

Preparing to read (Student's Book pg. 148)

THINKING ABOUT THE TOPIC

1 | Have students read the meanings of *deviance* and *crime* in a dictionary, then close their dictionaries while they do the next step.

2 | Explain that examples of deviant and criminal behavior will vary in different countries and cultures according to different laws and customs.

Sample answers
Deviant behavior is behavior that is regarded by society as outside acceptable norms or standards of behavior. *Criminal behavior* is behavior that is not only deviant, but also against the law.

3 | Draw students' attention to any cultural variations that become evident with relation to what is considered deviant and what is considered criminal.

4 | **Sample answers**
   • Use of the streets: deviant but not criminal – <u>crossing the street against a "Don't Walk" sign</u>
   • Use of alcohol: deviant and criminal – <u>driving while drunk</u>
   • Making money: deviant and criminal – <u>stealing</u>

5 | Elicit some views around the class.

Now read

Ask students to note the questions at the beginning of the text and answer them silently to themselves before they read on.

Refer to page xi of this Teacher's Manual for additional suggestions about ways in which students can read the text.

After you read (Student's Book pg. 151)

Task 1 BUILDING VOCABULARY: TECHNICAL TERMS AND DEFINITIONS

1 | Tell students to begin with the names of crimes that are most familiar to them. Encourage students to use each other as a resource to work out more difficult ones, and then, if necessary, to look up words in the dictionary.

Answers
Note that prostitution may not be a crime in some places.

<u>c</u> **1**

<u>f</u> **2**

<u>h</u> **3**

<u>l</u> **4**

<u>a</u> **5**

<u>d</u> **6**

<u>e</u> **7**

<u>j</u> **8**

<u>g</u> **9**

<u>b</u> **10**

2 | Use the same strategies as in step 1 to find the meanings for the crimes listed.

Sample answers
- *fraud:* Fraud is a crime in which someone gains an unfair advantage by being dishonest, that is, by lying or tricking other people.
- *tax evasion:* Tax evasion is a crime in which someone lies or does not report certain information to the government in order to avoid paying taxes.
- *embezzlement:* Embezzlement is a crime in which someone who is entrusted with looking after the money or possessions of another person takes that money for his or her own use, without permission to do so.

Task 2 UNDERSTANDING IMPLIED MEANINGS

Sample answers
1 Burglary doesn't involve an attack on a person, so it may seem to be a less serious or, perhaps, less dangerous crime. There may be less chance that a burglar could be identified. Burglary may allow the thief to steal more valuable goods.

2 Manual laborers traditionally wore blue work clothes, giving rise to the term "blue-collar worker." Male office workers and professionals wore a white shirt and tie, giving rise to the expression "white-collar worker." "White-collar crime" is nonviolent crime – usually theft, fraud, or embezzlement – committed by office workers and professionals against institutions, companies, or clients.

3 Some people have a fear of the police even when they have committed no crime. They may want to avoid publicity. They may think the police will not be able to help.

4 Homicide is mostly committed by people who know the victim. The weekend is the time that people spend together with family, friends, and acquaintances. Any tensions are more likely to surface during those times. Alcohol and other drugs may also play a part, and are more likely to be consumed on the weekend.

Task 3 PERSONALIZING THE TOPIC

The aim of this task is to make connections between the topic and students' lives. Don't be surprised if group discussions develop in a variety of directions.

2 WHO COMMITS CRIME?

Preparing to read (Student's Book pg. 152)

USING THE SQR3 SYSTEM

Ask for a volunteer to explain what *SQR3* stands for. Then read through the task commentary box to check the answer.

1 | Have students take careful note of the points under "Survey," then follow the strategies to survey the text. Elicit some comments on what they discovered.

2,3 | Have students compare the questions they write in the margins before they proceed to read the text with those same questions in mind.

Now read

Remind students to look for answers to the questions they wrote in the margins for step 2, "Question," of "Using the SQR3 System."

Refer to page xi of this Teacher's Manual for additional suggestions about ways in which students can read the text.

After you read (Student's Book pg. 156)

Task 1 USING THE SQR3 SYSTEM

1 | Direct partners to take turns giving oral summaries of the sections to each other.

2 | The review stage could be done in class or as a homework task.

Task 2 LANGUAGE FOCUS: COMPARING DATA

1 | **Answers**

  2 Older people have more relationships that encourage them to follow conventional behavior than younger people do.

  3 Men are more likely to be involved in the more profitable crimes of burglary and robbery than women are.

  4 It is less socially acceptable for females to be involved in crime.

  5 Men are under less social pressure to conform than women.

2 | **Answers**

  1 The rich are far less likely than the poor to be arrested.

  2 Criminal opportunities are still much less available to women than to men.

  3 People from lower socioeconomic groups in the community are more likely to be arrested than those from higher socioeconomic groups.

  4 Men are more likely to be selected and recruited into criminal groups.

Task 3 READING ACTIVELY

1 | Before they share their thoughts in a group, give students a minute or two to reflect individually.

2 | Ask groups to report back to the class on their discussions.

  Now that sections 1 and 2 have been completed, direct students to go back to the "Previewing the Unit" tasks for Chapter 7 on page 146 of the Student's Book to check the predictions they made.

3 COMPUTERS AND CRIME

Preparing to read (Student's Book pg. 158)

THINKING ABOUT THE TOPIC

1, 2 | There are no right or wrong answers to this task. The aim is to get students thinking about ideas and vocabulary associated with the topic, and to broaden their thinking on the topic by sharing ideas.

BUILDING VOCABULARY: LEARNING WORDS RELATED TO THE TOPIC

1 | **Answers**

Computers
- *Internet:* the electronic communications network that connects computers around the world and that allows people to communicate on-line
- *software:* the programs used by a computer as opposed to *hardware*, which is the physical components of a computer
- *homepage:* the main page, or site, of an address on the World Wide Web (WWW)
- *database:* a collection of data organized for rapid search and retrieval on a computer

Computer Crime
- *hacking:* getting into someone else's computer in order to steal information or cause damage
- *identify theft:* using information that identifies another person (such as a credit card number) to pretend you are that person, often for the purpose of stealing money
- *virus:* a hidden instruction in a computer program that is sent to other computers, sometimes with the purpose of destroying information on those computers
- *illegal copying:* making copies of computer programs or instructions for programs without permission from those who hold the copyright

2 | Elicit more words and meanings from the class.

Now read

Refer to page xi of this Teacher's Manual for suggestions about ways in which students can read the text.

After you read (Student's Book pg. 161)

Task 1 SUMMARIZING FROM THE MAIN IDEAS

1 | **Answers**

6	a
5	b
1, 2, 3, 4	c
BT	d

2 | Have students compare notes with a partner.

Sample answers
- using computers to solve crimes: computer databases of reported thefts; computer-transmitted photographs of suspects

- problems in fighting computer crime: many computer thefts from companies are not reported; difficulties for police in keeping up with technology
- kinds of computer crimes: stealing money; stealing software; stealing information through hacking; setting up fake companies; selling fake goods; sending viruses to attack other computers
- attitudes to computer crimes: Views are divided on whether it is wrong to use company computers and software for personal use.

3 | This task could be done in class or as a homework assignment.

Task 2 CONDUCTING A SURVEY

Read through the information in the task commentary box with your students.

1, 2 | While students are doing these steps, circulate around the class to offer assistance if needed. Have students practice asking and answering the questions. Make sure they take turns being the interviewer and interviewee.

3,4 | If possible, students should do these steps outside of class. Then have a student from each group report to the class on their findings.

4 TECHNIQUES FOR SOLVING CRIMES

Preparing to read (Student's Book pg. 162)

BRAINSTORMING

In preparation for the task, draw students' attention to the pictures on this page as well as to the illustration at the beginning of the text on page 163 of the Student's Book.

Have students work in small groups to share names and story lines of some television programs or movies about detectives solving crimes. Students may suggest traditional detective stories like Agatha Christie mysteries, or a modern TV police drama like *NYPD Blue*, or movies like *Gosford Park*. There are many possibilities.

1, 2 | Tell students they will have 5 minutes to brainstorm different ways to solve crimes. One member can record the ideas for each group. Have groups compare lists.

Sample answers
- secretly keeping watch on a suspect
- phone-tapping, that is, listening secretly to telephone conversations
- analysis of evidence found at the crime scene such as fingerprints, footprints, hair or fiber samples, or DNA on a glass
- matching handwriting
- finding a witness who saw what happened
- making a computer image of a suspect's face from a witness's description
- interviewing a suspect to get a confession

BUILDING BACKGROUND KNOWLEDGE OF THE TOPIC

1 | Have students read the description of DNA. They can look up the words *molecules* and *chromosomes* in a dictionary if they are not familiar with them. Many dictionaries and encyclopedias have simple illustrations of the DNA model, and it might be helpful for the students if you bring a copy of such an illustration to class.

2 | After pairs have discussed DNA's usefulness in solving crime, ask for volunteers to share their ideas with the class.

Now read

Refer to page xi of this Teacher's Manual for suggestions about ways in which students can read the text.

After you read (Student's Book pg. 165)

Task 1 UNDERSTANDING THE FUNCTION OF DIFFERENT PARTS OF A TEXT

Read through the task commentary box with students.

1 | Have students read over the list of functions.

2 | Examine lines 1 to 10 together as a class to make sure students understand the task. Have the students read quickly over those lines, and then discuss why "facts and explanations" is the correct answer. Circulate among the students as they do this task individually, giving help as needed. Check the answers with the whole class.

Answers

2 facts and explanations

3 past events

4 facts and explanations

5 discussion of an issue

6 facts and explanations

7 a point of view

8 data

Task 2 EXAMINING GRAPHIC MATERIAL

1 | **Answers**

2 Saliva on <u>gum</u> or a <u>cigarette butt</u> is more useful than that found on a <u>soda can</u> or <u>the ground</u>.

3 The least useful source of DNA is <u>that found on the handle of a knife or pistol found at the crime scene</u>.

4 Mucus on used tissue paper is not as useful as, for example, <u>a blood stain the size of a dime</u> or <u>a single hair with root and follicle</u> or <u>saliva on used gum or a cigarette butt</u>.

2 | **Sample answers**
- Skin cells on frequently worn clothing such as socks or gloves are a more useful source of DNA than skin cells on a doorknob.
- A single hair with root and follicle is much more useful than a hair without the root.
- Saliva on a soda can or mucus on a tissue both offer about the same likelihood of usable cells for determining DNA.

Task 3 WRITING A CHRONOLOGICAL PARAGRAPH

1 | Read the extract out loud to the class, giving emphasis to the underlined words.

2 | **Answers**

1 when
while

2 later
after
then

3 | Have students write notes in response to the questions. Students can write up their reports in class or for homework.

Chapter 7 WRITING ASSIGNMENT (Student's Book pg. 167)

Read through the topics with your students, eliciting from them which texts might be helpful to review prior to writing about each topic. You may want to put students who are going to write about the same topic in pairs or small groups to brainstorm ideas before they write and to give each other feedback afterwards.

Refer to the discussion of the Chapter 1 Writing Assignment on page 11 of this Teacher's Manual for further suggestions.

Controlling Crime

1 WHAT STOPS US FROM COMMITTING CRIMES?

Preparing to read (Student's Book pg. 168)

PERSONALIZING THE TOPIC

Remind students that the aim of the task is to have them relate the topic to their own lives and experiences, and that there are no right or wrong answers.

SPEED READING

Review the points in the task commentary box with the class. Then have students practice these techniques as they read the text. Give students a time limit of 4 minutes in which to read the text. After they read, give them time to exchange two or three main ideas with a partner.

Now read

Refer to page xi of this Teacher's Manual for suggestions about ways in which students can read the text.

After you read (Student's Book pg. 171)

Task 1 HIGHLIGHTING

Have students highlight the parts of the text. They can compare which parts they highlighted with a partner.

Task 2 LANGUAGE FOCUS: DESCRIBING INTERNAL AND EXTERNAL CONTROLS

Sample answers

A fear of being arrested discourages people from breaking the law.

A fear of being arrested stops drivers from speeding.

The threat of imprisonment prevents us from stealing.

The thought of my family finding out deters me from committing a crime.

Task 3 APPLYING WHAT YOU READ

Make sure students know that *plagiarism* means copying someone else's work and presenting it as your own. Have students review the parts of the text they highlighted in Task 1. They should think about those definitions and examples when discussing these questions.

Have students find out what the rules on plagiarism are in their school or college. Elicit their views on these rules. Are the punishments appropriate to the crime? Why or why not?

2 PRISONS

Preparing to read (Student's Book pg. 172)

READING AROUND THE TOPIC

1 | Provide some useful vocabulary to help students write about the data, for example: *percentage, smaller/smallest, larger/largest, lowest, highest, majority, less than, more than.*

Sample answers
- Prisoners who have been given a sentence of less than one year make up the smallest percentage of prisoners.
- The majority of prisoners are in prison for offenses related to drugs.
- Just over one-third of all prison inmates are in low-security prisons.

2 | After students discuss in pairs, elicit comments from the class.

THINKING ABOUT THE TOPIC

Students who have never visited a prison can think about what they have seen on television or in movies. Have a representative from each group summarize for the class some of the issues the group discussed.

Now read

Refer to page xi of this Teacher's Manual for suggestions about ways in which students can read the text.

After you read (Student's Book pg. 175)

Task 1 READING FOR DETAIL

Instruct students to read each question and then look back at the text for the answer. They can write the number of the question in the margin beside the relevant section of text, or make some notes on a piece of paper.

Elicit answers from the class one question at a time. Students should try to answer the questions without referring to the text or to their notes.

Answers

1 institutionalized prisoners who have been conditioned for prison from childhood; prisoners who were led to crime through economic and social circumstances; prisoners who are dedicated to a life of crime

2 to punish wrongdoers; to protect society or its citizens; to rehabilitate prisoners

3 educational or training programs; employment for prisoners in the prison; short-term work release outside the prison

4 prisons force people to be cut off from society; prisoners learn antisocial habits and attitudes in prison; prisoners mix with other criminals and learn new criminal skills

5 *Probation* means that a prisoner is allowed to remain in the community under supervision.

Task 2 BUILDING VOCABULARY: RECOGNIZING WORD "FAMILIES"

1 | This task is both a vocabulary-building activity as well as practice in scanning a text.

Answers
* deter   <u>deterrent</u> (par. 7)
* crime   <u>criminal</u> (par. 4)
* punishment <u>punish</u> (par. 5)
* homeless   <u>homelessness</u> (par. 3)
* rehabilitate <u>rehabilitation</u> (par. 7)

2 | **Answers**
1 homelessness

2 criminal

3 rehabilitation

4 rehabilitate *or* punish

5 deterrent

Task 3 APPLYING WHAT YOU READ

1 | Give students a time limit of 3 minutes to discuss each case. They should try to reach an agreement, although this may not be possible. Ask one member of each group to record the decision in each case, or the reason(s) for disagreement between group members. For each case, have the recorder from a different group report to the class on the group's decision, and on their disagreements, if any.

2 | Have students choose the case they think is most interesting or difficult in terms of deciding on a punishment. In explaining their opinion, they should take into account some of the different views expressed in step 1 by other students.

3 THE DEATH PENALTY

Preparing to read (Student's Book pg. 176)

PERSONALIZING THE TOPIC
After students have discussed in pairs, elicit some responses from the class. Make notes on the board of responses to question 3 and have students copy them or take their own notes. You will want the class to return to these notes when you do Task 3, Reading Critically, in "After You Read" on page 181 of the Student's Book.

SKIMMING

1 | **Answer**
b

2 | **Answer**
This text relies mostly on statistical data.

3 | Make sure partners have time to compare their findings.

Now read

Refer to page xi of this Teacher's Manual for suggestions about ways in which students can read the text.

After you read (Student's Book pg. 180)

Task 1 READING FOR DETAIL
Ask students to do this task individually, referring back to the relevant parts of the text when necessary. They can then compare answers with a partner.

1 In states that have abolished capital punishment, the murder rates <u>are generally much lower than in states that still have capital punishment</u>.

2 When some states returned to using the death penalty, <u>it did not lead to any significant decrease in homicides</u>.

3 After widely publicized executions of criminals in Philadelphia in the 1930s, <u>there was no change in the number of homicides</u>.

4 The evidence from other countries <u>shows that when the death penalty was abolished, there was often a decrease in the number of homicides</u>.

2 | **Answers**

There was widespread public support for the death penalty in the 1990s. The decline since 1999 may reflect a shift in public opinion.

Task 2 BUILDING VOCABULARY: SYNONYMS

Sample answers

- death penalty   <u>capital punishment</u>

- homicide   <u>murder</u>

- deter   <u>discourage</u>

- go up   <u>increase</u>

- decline   <u>decrease</u>

- accurately   <u>precisely/correctly</u>

- powerful   <u>strong</u>

- preventing   <u>stopping</u>

- outrage   <u>anger</u>

- advocate   <u>support</u>

Task 3 READING CRITICALLY

Have students review the notes they made in "Personalizing the Topic" on page 176 of the Student's Book and then discuss the questions for this task with a partner. Remind them that they can review ideas and examples from the text to assist the discussion.

Task 4 CONDUCTING A SURVEY

1 | Before students look back to page 161 to review the points on preparing survey questions, see if they can recall some of the points from memory.

2 | Have students begin their data collection in class by asking each other the questions. They should then try to collect more data outside of class.

3,4 | Ask each student to calculate their results and then to write several statements to report their findings. Have students compare their results with those of several other students.

4 THE WAR ON DRUGS

Preparing to read (Student's Book pg. 182)

BUILDING VOCABULARY: LEARNING WORDS RELATED TO THE TOPIC

1,2 | **Answers**

- *the war on drugs:* The metaphor of "war" is often used to describe the fight against drugs.

- *the drug problem:* negative issues and behaviors associated with drug use

- *drug dealing:* selling drugs

- *drug addicts:* people who have become physically dependent on drugs

- *drug related homicides:* murders related to drugs

- *drug overdose:* taking so much of a drug as to cause physical harm or even death

- *drug education programs:* programs to teach people about the negative effects of drugs

- *drug treatment:* methods and programs to help drug addicts overcome their problem

- *drug abuse:* using a drug in a way that can cause harmful effects or addiction

- *legalization of drugs:* changes to the law so that drug use is not illegal

PREDICTING

Ask students to discuss their predictions in a group. Elicit views from several groups before asking students to read the text.

Now read

Refer to page xi of this Teacher's Manual for suggestions about ways in which students can read the text.

After you read (Student's Book pg. 185)

Task 1 NOTE TAKING: MAKING A CHART

1 | If possible, have students use two different colored highlighters to do this task. They should highlight arguments *for* in one color, and arguments *against* in another.

2 | Draw a chart on the board or on an overhead transparency with a column headed "For" and a column headed "Against." Have students copy the chart into their notebooks and record the relevant arguments in note form.

Answers (*not* in note form)
Arguments for the legalization of drugs:
- The current laws do more harm than good. For example, police spend time arresting people for smoking marijuana rather than arresting robbers or murders.
- The high cost of illegal drugs causes drug users and addicts to commit crimes more serious than drug use – for example, robbery or burglary – in order to afford drugs.
- The huge amounts of money spent on enforcing drug laws could be used for drug treatment and education.
- By making drugs illegal, the government is violating individual rights.

Arguments against the legalization of drugs:
- If drugs become legal, drug use will skyrocket. The repeal of Prohibition in the United States is an example. When Prohibition ended, in 1933, the use of alcohol apparently soared by 350 percent.
- Use of milder drugs, such as marijuana, lead to use of harder drugs, such as heroin and cocaine. If drugs were legal, more people would use milder drugs and then go on to use harder drugs.
- The government should protect people from harming themselves.

3 | Have students return to the predictions they made before they read the text (Predicting, on page 182 of the Student's Book) to compare those predictions with the notes they recorded above.

Task 2 VARYING YOUR LANGUAGE

1 | Have students find and highlight in the text the words in the three lists. Elicit one or two other words that could be added to the appropriate list.

2 | **Sample answers**

1 are in favor of

2 think

3 causes

4 argue

5 lead to

6 encourage

7 believe

8 feel

9 are in favor of

10 believe

11 think

12 lead

13 propose

14 cause

3 | Ask students to do this task individually. It can be done in class or as a homework task. Have students exchange and read each other's completed paragraphs.

Task 3 BUILDING VOCABULARY: FIGURATIVE LANGUAGE

1 | Begin by having students look at the illustrations and try to guess the figurative expression each represents. Then they can check themselves by looking in the paragraphs indicated.

Answers

2 look the other way

3 skyrocket

4 stepping stone

5 the root causes of the problem

2 | Have partners take turns explaining what the expressions mean. Then you might ask for volunteers to use some of the expressions in other appropriate contexts.

Chapter 8 WRITING ASSIGNMENT (Student's Book pg. 188)

Read through the topics with your students, eliciting from them which texts might be helpful to review prior to writing about each topic. You may want to put students who are going to write about the same topic in pairs or small groups to brainstorm ideas before they write and to give each other feedback afterwards.

Refer to the discussion of the Chapter 1 Writing Assignment on page 11 of this Teacher's Manual for further suggestions.

Changing Societies

Unit title page (Student's Book pg. 189)

Write the title of the unit, "Changing Societies," on the board and underneath it list the following key words and expressions from the introductory paragraph:

from place to place	the workplace	cities
over time	our whole planet	environment
technology	population	the future

In groups, have students discuss some issues, suggested by the key words, that they expect to find discussed in the unit.

Previewing the unit (Student's Book pg. 190)

Chapter 9: Cultural change

Elicit responses from the class and note some suggestions on the board. An interesting question to raise is whether both these photographs could have been taken in the same city. This may give rise to discussion about what *culture* means, and whether there are cultural differences within as well as across societies.

Sample answers
Students may suggest differences in
- dress codes
- gender roles, especially in relation to child care and shopping
- ways of buying and selling goods; differences between individual market stalls and supermarkets

The discussion may also extend to issues of bargaining in shopping.

Chapter 10: Global issues

Have students begin this task individually. Once they have made predictions for each question, they can compare their ideas with a partner. Tell students that they will find out whether their predictions were correct as they read through Chapter 10. Do not correct students' answers at this point.

Answers
_a_ **1**

_b_ **2**

_c_ **3**

_b_ **4**

_d_ **5**

Chapter 9

Cultural change

1 CULTURAL VARIATION AND CHANGE

Preparing to read (Student's Book pg. 192)

PREVIEWING ART IN THE TEXT

1 | Explain, if necessary, that the word *caption* means the small text under a picture that explains what the picture is about.

2,3 | **Answers**
- What is culture?: pictures on page 193
- Cultural variation: pictures on page 194
- How cultures change: pictures on page 195

THINKING ABOUT THE TOPIC

1 | Give students time to discuss in pairs, and then elicit some comments from the class. Do not correct any suggestions at this point, but tell students that they will read more about the meaning of *culture*.

2 | Remind students that to *skim* means to look quickly over the text to get the main ideas. This can be a fun task as students will discover some unusual ways to get married.

3 | Give students time to discuss in pairs, then elicit some examples of cultural changes from the class.

Now read

Refer to page xi of this Teacher's Manual for suggestions about ways in which students can read the text.

After you read (Student's Book pg. 196)

Task 1 SHARING YOUR CULTURAL PERSPECTIVE

Draw students' attention to the recycling sign and the accompanying paragraph. Discuss the idea that the sign means recycling, but that as a symbol it represents a much broader meaning. We could say that it is a symbol of a broad set of values or beliefs about the need to take care of the environment.

1,2 | First, discuss what each picture shows. Then ask students to think about what each one symbolizes. Note that some pictures can symbolize more than one thing, and meanings may vary across cultures.

Sample answers

1 wristwatch: the importance of time/punctuality/deadlines; the pressure of time in modern life

2 wheelchair access sign: an inclusive society that provides for difference, including difference in physical ability; care for the disabled

3 rocket launch: the value of science and technology; a desire to understand more about the universe

4 "No Smoking" sign: a concern for people's health and an awareness of the dangers of smoking; the belief that we need laws to keep people from harming themselves

3 | If students are unable to make suggestions, you could add other examples such as a credit card or a supermarket cart. Draw pictures of artifacts on the board (or bring pictures to class). Then, in groups, have students discuss what they symbolize.

Task 2 SUMMARIZING FROM TOPIC SENTENCES

1 | Read the topic sentences out loud to students while they follow the written version. Be sure that students understand that the word *homogeneous* means "all of the same kind."

2 | Have students identify with a partner the changes made in the summary. If possible, put a copy of the original and edited versions on an overhead transparency so that you can point to the editing changes as you discuss them with the class.

3 | Put the introductory sentence on the board and ask students how they think the text should continue. Write the second sentence suggested by students on the board. Then have students finish writing the summary paragraph individually.

Sample answer

All cultures change over time as a result of a number of factors. Some changes come about through variation within a culture, whereas others are a result of the introduction of new technologies, or of different cultures coming into contact with and borrowing from each other. Public discussion and debate in the media or in the process of political elections can also bring about change in cultural values and norms.

4 | Ask students to give their paragraph to a partner to read. Provide some guidelines for the kind of feedback students can give to their partner. For example, suggest that they use the following checklist of questions:
- Have all the main ideas been included?
- Does the paragraph flow smoothly from one idea to the next?
- Is there any unnecessary repetition of words or ideas?
- Are corrections needed in grammar, spelling, or punctuation?

Task 3 READING ACTIVELY
Have each group give a brief report on some issues they discussed.

2 SUBCULTURES AND CULTS

Preparing to read (Student's Book pg. 198)

THINKING ABOUT THE TOPIC

1 | Ask students to make a list of at least four groups that they belong to. Then, in small groups, they can compare their answers and give examples of the particular language, clothes, or behaviors of each group. Students may suggest groups based on age, ethnicity, religion, language, gender, or social roles such as family member, student, or supporter of a particular sport or sporting team.

2 | Draw students' attention to the picture and elicit any vocabulary they know related to surfing. They may know, for example, *surfers, wet suits, surfboards*, and *waves*. Discuss as a class ways that the surfing subculture might differ from the larger culture. Students may suggest differences in clothes, hairstyles, or special language. Explain that they will read more about subcultures.

Sample answers
- other sport or leisure subcultures
- subcultures based on involvement with certain kinds of music
- subcultures based on styles of dress

3 | Elicit what students know about the group shown in the photograph. They may know that the people are members of Hare Krishna, a cult based on worship of the Hindu god Krishna. Even though students may not know the names of other cults, they might be able to describe what the cults are like. Explain that they will read more about cults.

Now read

Refer to page xi of this Teacher's Manual for suggestions about ways in which students can read the text.

After you read (Student's Book pg. 201)

Task 1 READING FOR DETAIL

Have students check the text for the answers to the questions. Encourage them to discuss any examples related to their personal experience.

Sample answers

1 Some values of one subculture may conflict with values of another, so that being a member of both subcultures can cause personal conflict.

2 Global youth cultures have resulted from the influence of globally broadcast television shows, movies, and video clips, as well as international music and sporting stars. Technology now allows young people all over the world to keep in touch with changing global influences.

3 Cults always have a charismatic leader. Cult members are usually young, middle-class, and looking for a new philosophy or way of life as a result of some dissatisfaction with their lives.

4 Cults put enormous pressure on people to stay in the cult. Some people claim that cults even use mind control and brainwashing techniques.

Task 2 WRITING EXPANDED DEFINITIONS

Review with the students the examples of expanded definitions in Chapter 2, in Task 2 on pages 32–33 of the Student's Book.

1 **Sample answer**
Subcultures are groups within a larger culture that are different from the larger culture in some values or behaviors. These differences can cause conflict for a person who belongs to more than one subculture.

2 **Sample answer**
Youth subcultures are sometimes described as tribes. Today's youth can belong to global tribes because of the influence of new technologies, such as satellite television and the Internet. These technologies keep young people around the world in touch with the latest trends.

3 **Sample answer**
Cults are sometimes religious or quasi-religious groups. They have charismatic leaders, and their members are usually young and middle-class. Some cults have been accused of brainwashing members to discourage them from leaving the cult.

4 Circulate through the class, offering help as needed, while students compare their definitions with partners.

Task 3 PERSONALIZING THE TOPIC

Ask students to reflect for a moment on their own situation. Ask for a show of hands of those who would answer "a lot," "somewhat," "very little," or "not at all" to the question of whether or not they belong to a global culture. Use the points listed to prompt discussion of aspects of their lives that they see as part of a global culture.

⓷ CHANGING COMMUNICATION

Preparing to read (Student's Book pg. 202)

PERSONALIZING THE TOPIC

1,2 | Have students complete the table. Then they can compare their responses with others in the class. Elicit feedback from the class to find the most frequently used channel(s) for communicating with friends and for study. Discuss the reasons for this.

THINKING ABOUT THE TOPIC

Draw students' attention to the photographs, but explain that these are prompts only and that their discussions can go beyond what they see in the photographs. Suggest that they also look ahead to other photographs in the section. Ask some pairs of students to report on their discussion to the class.

Now read

Refer to page xi of this Teacher's Manual for suggestions about ways in which students can read the text.

After you read (Student's Book pg. 205)

Task 1 BUILDING VOCABULARY: DESCRIPTIVE WORDS

1 | **Answers**
  • frequent and flexible: e-mail and cell-phone communication
  • trivial and mundane: much of the communication we have with family and friends
  • isolated and alienated: the feeling we can get from city life
  • wanted, needed, and loved: the feeling we can get from a phone call or an e-mail message

2 | Have students discuss meanings with a partner before they check them in a dictionary.

3 | Answers

1 convenient

2 inconsiderate

3 motivating, valuable *or* important

Task 2 LANGUAGE FOCUS: WRITING ABOUT POSSIBILITIES

1 | Answer
Sentence 1 implies that it is possible but not very certain that he would practice his English. Sentence 2 implies a high degree of certainty.

2 | Sample answers
If she had a computer, she would e-mail her friends every day.

If she had access to the Internet, she could order her textbooks on-line.

If she had a cell phone, she could make calls while she was walking to work.

3 Have students make some notes as they discuss the questions with a partner. The notes will help them do step 4, below.

4 Write the opening sentence on the board and elicit a list of some of the social and cultural consequences. The paragraph can be completed in class or as a homework task. Students can exchange completed drafts with a partner and give feedback on whether or not they agree with the ideas expressed.

4 THE CHANGING WORKPLACE

Preparing to read (Student's Book pg. 206)

PERSONALIZING THE TOPIC

1,2 When students have completed the table, have them tell their partners more about their chosen job.

3 Have students discuss these questions in small groups. Then conduct a poll by show of hands. Ask who would answer **a** and who would answer **b** to the question about an ideal job. Discuss the reasons for their answers.

Now read

Refer to page xi of this Teacher's Manual for suggestions about ways in which students can read the text.

After you read (Student's Book pg. 209)

Task 1 UNDERSTANDING THE FUNCTION OF DIFFERENT PARTS OF THE TEXT

1 | Have students skim the text one paragraph at a time, then find the matching function. Suggest that if students find one paragraph difficult, they should skip to the next and return to the difficult one later.

Answers

<u>par. 2</u>: It describes the difference between present and past attitudes to work.

<u>par. 6</u>: It predicts how working conditions in the future will be different from the present.

<u>par. 3</u>: It explains why there is a different attitude to work today than in the past.

<u>par. 1</u>: It gives a personal example of one individual's modern working lifestyle.

<u>par. 4</u>: It gives some examples of how present-day workplace conditions are different from the past.

<u>par. 5</u>: It describes a change in the types of work available today.

2 | Students will probably need guidance in order to understand what is being asked of them in this step. You might give them the first answer – about beginning with a personal example – and then ask what the writer is doing in the second paragraph. Encourage students to find the answers by thinking about what the writer is doing in each paragraph. Offer help as needed.

Sample answers
- By beginning with a personal example, the writer makes the issue seem more interesting and relevant to the reader.
- The writer makes the first main point about changes in attitudes to work.
- This is followed by an explanation of how these changes in attitude came about.
- The writer then makes the second main point about changes in workplace conditions.
- This is followed by the third main point about changes in types of work available.
- Finally, the writer looks to the future.

3 | **Answer**
These sentences could be placed at the end of paragraph 5. They discuss another example of changes in types of jobs.

Task 2 BUILDING VOCABULARY: USING CONTEXT CLUES

1,2 | **Answers**
1 commute

2 reject

3 substantially

4 flexible

5 profits

6 leisure

7 expect, foresee

8 problems, challenges

Task 3 PUNCTUATION

1,2 | **Sample answers**

- comma: (par. 1) "At least twice a week, he works from his Ohio home on a computer that is linked to his office." The comma separates a time phrase that occurs before the subject of the sentence from the main clause.
- question mark: (par. 3) "How has this new work ethic come about?" This is a rhetorical question, that is, one that does not expect a response from the reader, but poses a question that the writer will go on to answer.
- dash: (par. 1) "to commute in the usual way – by car or public transportation." The dash signals that the following text offers examples of "the usual way."
- quotation marks: (par. 1) "Vince says, 'We have to attend a lot of training sessions.'" The quotation marks indicate that these are someone's exact words.
- parentheses: (par. 3) " . . . three times as many white-collar workers (professionals, office workers, and sales people) as blue-collar workers . . . " The parentheses indicate that the ideas are not part of the main body of the text. This is additional information that could be omitted without disrupting the main point.
- colon and semi-colon: (par. 4) " . . . working conditions that will keep them happy: more interesting and varied tasks; more opportunities for self-direction; more flexible hours . . . " The colon signals the beginning of a list, and the semi-colon signals the separation of items in the list.

3 | **Answer**

It may be extremely important to have a job**,** but does it bring happiness**?** **In** many studies over the last two decades**,** workers have been asked whether they would continue to work if they inherited enough money to live comfortably without working**.** **M**ore than 70 percent replied that they would**.** **A**sked how satisfied they were with their jobs, even more **–** 80 to 90 percent **–** replied that they were very or moderately satisfied**.** **B**ut asked whether they would choose the same line of work if they could begin all over again, most said**, "No." O**nly 43 percent of white-collar workers and 24 percent of blue-collar workers said**, "Yes."** **A**nd when asked**, "D**o you enjoy your work so much that you have a hard time putting it aside**?"**, only 34 percent of men and 32 percent of women said**, "Yes."** **In** short**,** most people seem to like their jobs**,** but are not too excited about them.

Chapter 9 WRITING ASSIGNMENT (Student's Book pg. 211)

Ask students to look over the topic choices for one that interests them. Topic 4 requires students to collect data. For other topics it may be useful for students to look for some additional information in a library or on the Internet. You may want to put students who are going to write about the same topic in pairs or small groups to brainstorm ideas before they write and to give each other feedback afterwards.

Refer to the discussion of the Chapter 1 Writing Assignment on page 11 of this Teacher's Manual for further suggestions.

Global Issues

1 POPULATION CHANGE

Preparing to read (Student's Book pg. 212)

READING AROUND THE TOPIC

Before reading through the boxed text, read through the questions underneath it with students, so that they will have an idea of what to look for when they read. Be sure students understand the meaning of the word *pattern* in questions 1 and 2.

For questions 1 and 2, students must, to some extent, infer the answers based on the many statistics in the boxed text. Elicit reasons for their inferences.

In answering questions 3, 4, and 5, students will, of course, vary in their knowledge of exact statistics about their own or other countries, but they are likely to have a general idea of population trends. You might want to prepare yourself for these questions by researching the population and fertility rate statistics for the particular countries your students come from.

SKIMMING

1,2 | Elicit as much information as possible from students in order to make the point that they have learned a considerable amount by simply skimming the text.

Answers

1 The first sentence in the first paragraph explains what the pattern of human population growth has been: "For the past million years the world's population has grown almost continuously, although not always at the same rate." The first sentence of the second paragraph expands on this by explaining that although the growth has been continuous, the majority of it has happened in three great surges.

2 The first sentence of paragraph 3 explains that a change is predicted in this pattern: the world's population may begin to stabilize. The first sentence of paragraph 6 gives some information about why this stabilization may occur: the world fertility rate – the number of children per woman – is declining.

Now read

Refer to page xi of this Teacher's Manual for suggestions about ways in which students can read the text.

After you read (Student's Book pg. 216)

Task 1 READING FOR DETAIL

Students will have to read the text very closely to complete the chart, and they will have to make connections between sentences as well as within sentences. They will also have to do some numerical calculations.

You may need to explain that *AD* refers to the way of counting years since the birth of Christ. (*Anno* means "year" and *Domini* means "Lord," that is, Christ.) The years before Christ's birth are referred to as *BC* ("before Christ").

Answers

Year	Population
10,000 years ago	less than 10 million
1 AD	150 million
1000 AD	350 million
1800 AD	1 billion
1930 AD	2 billion
1960 AD	3 billion
2000 AD	6 billion
2100 AD	10 billion

Task 2 LANGUAGE FOCUS: REFERRING BACK TO IDEAS IN THE TEXT

Emphasize the importance of keeping track of pronouns and other words used to refer back to ideas previously mentioned. A reference could be not only to an idea in a previous sentence but also to an idea in a previous paragraph. You might also encourage students to be alert for references to ideas that will occur in future clauses or sentences.

1, 2 | Answers

2 technological revolution

3 the industrial revolution (the third technological revolution)

4 the second demographic stage

5 the third demographic stage

6 children

7 the problem (in relation to famine)

Task 3 EXPLAINING THE TEXT IN YOUR OWN WORDS

Review the "Recite" part of the SQR3 approach, which is explained in Task 1 on page 89 of the Student's Book.

1, 2 Encourage students to use the information in Figure 10.1 and Table 10.1 as well as the information in the text to answer the questions.

Sample answers

1 Each of the three great population surges happened after a technological revolution: the tool-making revolution, the farming – or agricultural – revolution, and the industrial revolution. This is because each revolution dramatically increased the number of people that the world could keep alive.

2 Social factors help to determine the number of children people have. For example, in poor, rural societies children are needed to work the fields and take care of their elderly parents. In cities, however, children aren't needed in this way and are also costly to educate, clothe, and feed. Also, as medical care has improved, more children stay alive to adulthood and so people do not need to have so many babies to ensure that some survive.

3 The fertility rate is declining overall, but it varies from country to country. Rates are still high in developing countries and very low in developed ones.

4 The doomsday theorists say that the world will run out of food and millions of people will die of starvation. Their opponents say that the shortage of food today has more to do with social and economic factors, such as war and poverty.

Task 4 READING ACTIVELY

1 Encourage students to go beyond the statistics and look for information about past trends and the factors that caused them. Ask them to think about which social and economic trends today might affect population, and in which ways.

2 Be aware that the culturally and religiously sensitive issue of birth control is likely to come up in this discussion.

2 FLIGHT TO THE CITIES

Preparing to read (Student's Book pg. 218)

THINKING ABOUT THE TOPIC

1 After students read the task, check which cities they have decided to make notes about. If many students are doing the same city, you could encourage some to choose a different one.

2 | Try to pair students who have chosen different cities first. It will also be interesting, however, for students to see how their opinions of the positive and negative aspects of the same city compare.

3 | Encourage students to ask each other for reasons to support their views.

PREPARING FOR A SHORT-ANSWER TEST

Make sure students understand that they only have to look for where the answers might occur. They are not expected to actually be able to answer the questions at this point.

Now read

Refer to page xi of this Teacher's Manual for suggestions about ways in which students can read the text.

After you read (Student's Book pg. 222)

Task 1 WRITING SHORT ANSWERS TO TEST QUESTIONS

1, 2 | Make sure that students do the highlighting part of this task. Give them adequate time to fully understand the relevant parts of the text. In order to simulate more closely what would happen in an authentic academic context, don't discuss the questions or give students any help in writing their answers.

Sample Answers

1 One of the following:
   - Conditions of city life, such as population density and great social diversity, harm the inhabitants by causing alienation and stress.
   - No matter what size the city is, people get involved in a small circle of friends and relatives. The personal lives of urban people are not that much different from those who live in rural areas.
   - Urban living enriches lives, for example, by creating diverse opportunities and strengthening subcultures.
   - One theory does not cover the whole situation. Most people value the positive aspects of city living and put up with the negative aspects.

2 The study of New Yorkers shows that they hate some aspects of living in New York, but are prepared to put up with these so that they can take advantage of the positive aspects.

3 Three reasons people move to cities are the following:
   - There are more jobs and/or higher wages in cities.
   - Rural areas are becoming less attractive due to environmental damage.
   - Cities have good support services, such as roads, schools, and hospitals.

4 A megacity is a city with a population of more than 10 million.

5 Problems of megacities include traffic, air pollution, and garbage disposal.

6 One of the following:

- Tokyo has improved its air standards with increased use of public transport and antipollution technology.
- New York has cleaned up its streets and waterways.
- São Paulo is creating a bicycle system to reduce traffic congestion.

Task 2 LANGUAGE FOCUS: NOMINALIZATIONS

Read through the task commentary box with students. Mention that nominalization is more commonly used in formal written texts than in informal ones or in spoken language. Explain that it is more difficult to understand texts that are heavily nominalized because of the way they allow the writer to "pack" the meanings in tightly, creating a dense and abstract text.

Students need to be aware of the importance of using nominalization in their own academic writing. The more control they have over the nominalization process, the more appropriate their academic writing will be.

1 Encourage students to reword sentences in which nominalizations occur and begin them in a different way. Circulate among the pairs, offering help as needed.

2 Review students' answers in class. Draw their attention to the whole structure of the nominalized sentences and the different reasons the writer could have for choosing nominalized over non-nominalized forms.

Answers

2 alienation

3 Homelessness

4 diversity

5 congestion

6 tension

Task 3 PERSONAL WRITING

Refer students back to "Thinking About the Topic" on page 218 of the Student's Book. The notes and discussion relevant to that activity could be a useful starting point for their personal writing.

3 THE ENVIRONMENT

Preparing to read (Student's Book pg. 224)

THINKING ABOUT THE TOPIC

1 Have students quickly read through the questionnaire to make sure they understand all the questions before completing it.

2 Have students count up their "yes" responses to determine how planet-friendly they are. It is likely that students wanted to qualify some answers, so encourage discussion of their responses to reveal any qualifications.

3 Encourage students to be specific in their responses to each of the two questions. Ask them to give examples where possible.

Now read

Refer to page xi of this Teacher's Manual for suggestions about ways in which students can read the text.

After you read (Student's Book pg. 228)

Task 1 READING FOR THE MAIN IDEA

1 When checking answers, explain that the correct answer, although very broadly stated, captures all the main ideas in the text to some extent.

Answer
b

2 **Answer**
c

Task 2 THINKING ABOUT THE TOPIC

You might want to suggest that students copy the headings and fill in the chart on a separate piece of paper.

1 **Sample answer**

Good news	Bad news
• some say environment will be better in the future because we will know better how to control it, and technology will provide us with new resources	• DDT used to protect crops but ended up in soil and water, and then our food
• great awareness of need to save environment	• soon we might run out of some basic resources
• there are now a number of "green" political parties	• global supply of oil might only last 50 years
• organizations such as Greenpeace are being asked for advice	• we are losing topsoil at an alarming rate
• Kyoto Protocol to fight global warming	• air pollution from automobiles – accounts for 80% of air pollution
• some signs that the ozone hole may be starting to repair itself	• global warming as a result of industrial pollution – may cause worldwide flooding
• some countries working hard to preserve environment, for example, Suriname	• hole in the ozone layer
• individual actions at home and workplace	

2 | Encourage students to give specific reasons for their answers to both questions. In response to question 2, students may mention programs they know about that are working to improve the environment. If so, tell them that this information will be relevant to Task 4, "Writing a Problem-Solution Text."

Task 3 UNDERSTANDING LINKING OF IDEAS

Discuss the task commentary box. Explain the importance of understanding the relationship between sentences in order to comprehend the details in the text and the need to understand the link even when it is not explicitly stated.

Answers

<u>c</u> **2**

<u>b</u> **3**

<u>b</u> **4**

<u>a</u> **5**

Task 4 WRITING A PROBLEM-SOLUTION TEXT

Discuss the task commentary box. Explain that problem-solution texts often have many sentences and paragraphs that express cause and effect relationships. You might want to refer back to Task 2, "Reading Critically," on page 142, in which ways to express cause and effect relationships are noted.

1 | Refer students back to their discussions about the environment in step 2 of Task 2, "Thinking About the Topic," before beginning this group discussion.

2 | This could be a homework assignment, allowing students more time to do some further research, if needed. Be sure they understand that they should include some possible solutions as well as an explanation of the actual problem. Encourage students to use some of the main ideas from the text in their writing.

4 INTO THE FUTURE

Preparing to read (Student's Book pg. 230)

THINKING ABOUT THE TOPIC

1,2 | Ask students to give reasons for their opinions. Encourage them to give evidence for each possibility. Make the discussion as lively as possible by encouraging debate where students differ in their opinions.

SKIMMING

Answers

1 present

2 demographic *or* population

3 social

    4 technology

    5 science

    6 certain

    7 planets

Now read

Refer to page xi of this Teacher's Manual for suggestions about ways in which students can read the text.

After you read (Student's Book pg. 233)

Task 1 READING FOR DETAIL

1 | **Answers**

| **1** Decrease | **3** Increase | **5** Increase | **7** Decrease |
| **2** Decrease | **4** Increase | **6** Increase | **8** Increase |

2 | **Answers**

  F **1**

  T **2**

  T **3**

  T **4**

  T **5**

  F **6**

  T **7**

3 | Circulate among pairs, helping as needed. Be sure that students justify their answers.

Task 2 LANGUAGE FOCUS: VERBS TO USE INSTEAD OF "SAY" AND "WRITE"

Read through the commentary box with the students. You might brainstorm other words to add to the list.

1 | **Answers**
- par. 2: predict
- par. 3: comment
       suggest
- par. 4: think
- par. 5: think
       comment
- boxed text: believe
          warn

2 | Answers

1 warned, predicted

2 explain, discuss

3 predicted

4 argue, believe; disagree

5 believe, think

6 identifies/identified, lists/listed, discusses/discussed, points to/pointed to

7 explained

8 predict, believe, agree, warn

9 comments/commented, asserts/asserted

10 estimate

Task 3 CONDUCTING A SURVEY

1 | Allow time for discussion of the issue before doing a "hands-up" survey.

2 | Work through each bullet point to prepare the survey. You may want to review the information about conducting a survey in the commentary box for Task 2, "Conducting a Survey," on page 161, in Chapter 7.

3 | You could keep the in-class results separate from the outside-class results or you could combine them. "Write up the findings" can be a whole class activity.

4 | Give the class a few minutes to review the results reported in the boxed text. Then ask for volunteers to compare those results with the results gathered by the class.

Before discussing the Chapter 10 Writing Assignment, ask students to refer back to their answers to the questions about Chapter 10 in "Previewing the Unit" on page 190 of the Student's Book. Give them time to review their answers and adjust them, if necessary, based on what they learned from Chapter 10. Discuss the answers as a class.

Chapter 10 WRITING ASSIGNMENT (Student's Book pg. 235)

Ask students to look over the choices for one that interests them. Topic 3 is a general question about the future that gives students a chance to use information from other chapters of the text as well as from Chapter 10. Elicit ideas about which chapters and sections might be relevant to the areas of activity listed here. You may want to put students who are going to write about the same topic in pairs or small groups to brainstorm ideas before they write and to give each other feedback afterwards.

Refer to the discussion of the Chapter 1 Writing Assignment on page 11 of this Teacher's Manual for further suggestions.

Unit 1 CONTENT QUIZ

PART 1 True/False questions (24 points)

Decide if the following statements are true (T) or false (F).

_____ 1 A man and a woman who live together as a couple (cohabit) don't usually get married to one another.

_____ 2 Children are socialized in much the same way all around the world.

_____ 3 Feral children provide evidence of the importance of nurture in the nature-nurture debate.

_____ 4 A rule about not eating a certain food in a particular culture is a good example of a taboo.

_____ 5 A football crowd is an example of a conventional crowd.

_____ 6 Panic is a rational reaction to extreme danger.

PART 2 Multiple choice questions (24 points)

Circle the best answer from the choices listed.

1 The percentage of married women in the workforce in the United States
   a has increased a little since 1960.
   b has increased by 10% since 1960.
   c has almost doubled since 1960.
   d has tripled since 1960.

2 Our intelligence and aptitude
   a are inherited from our parents.
   b are determined through socialization.
   c may be limited or improved by socialization.
   d are not limited by either nature or nurture.

3 Folkways, taboos, and mores are all different forms of
   a socialization.
   b cultural norms.
   c cultural behaviors.
   d social values.

4 The emergent-norm theory of crowd behavior says that
   a there is great social pressure on individuals to behave like others in a crowd, even when they may not agree with the crowd behavior.
   b although there are different kinds of crowds, all crowds share a few characteristics.
   c because we are faceless and nameless in a crowd, we can let our primitive side show.
   d in crowds, people often behave in a way that is different from their normal, everyday way of behavior.

PART 3 Short answer questions (24 points)

Write a short answer to each of the following questions. In most cases no more than one or two sentences is required.

1 What is the difference between cohabitation and communal living?

2 What are positive and negative sanctions? Give an example of each.

3 Why is running away from a burning house *not* an example of "panic"?

PART 4 One paragraph or short essay answer (28 points)

Choose one of the following topics and write a paragraph or short essay about it. Use a separate sheet of paper.

1 New forms of family units and lifestyles in the United States and other countries today

2 The influence of the adolescent peer group

Unit **2** CONTENT QUIZ

PART 1 True/False questions (24 points)

Decide if the following statements are true (T) or false (F).

_____ **1** Gender-neutral socialization is more popular with mothers than fathers.

_____ **2** In general, there are still more male characters in children's books than female characters.

_____ **3** Girls have more social problems than boys while they are at school and after they leave school.

_____ **4** When a man and a woman marry, the man gains approximately half the amount of household work that the woman does.

_____ **5** The United States has one of the worst records among industrial nations in relation to women's earnings compared to men's.

_____ **6** One explanation for "sex role spillover" is that we define people more by their gender than by their work.

PART 2 Multiple choice questions (24 points)

Circle the best answer from the choices listed.

1 One reason that women in traditional fairy tales are quiet and passive is that
  a the writers were usually male.
  b the fairy tales have been translated from stories in other cultures.
  c this is the way women were expected to behave when these stories were written.
  d the writers were more interested in creating strong male characters.

2 The structure of most schools in the United States
  a can send out a message that girls are less important than boys.
  b suggests that more women should try to become school principals.
  c suggests that men will always take leadership roles in the workplace.
  d can send out a message that women need men to lead them.

3 Over the past few decades, female gender roles in the media
  a have changed dramatically.
  b have changed in some ways but traditional stereotypes still persist.
  c have not changed at all.
  d have changed in magazines but not in TV programs.

4 Paying people to do housework
  a is likely to happen as more pressure is applied to governments around the world.
  b is unlikely to happen because of the difficulties involved in establishing a system for payment.
  c has already been introduced in Australia.
  d is an idea mostly supported by women.

PART 3 Short answer questions (24 points)

Write a short answer to each of the following questions. In most cases no more than one or two sentences is required.

1 Give one reason why it can be difficult for parents to bring up boys and girls in the same way.

2 Why do men feel such a loss of self-esteem when they lose their jobs?

3 What are two arguments *against* putting sexual harassment laws and policies in place in the workplace.

PART 4 One paragraph or short essay answer (28 points)

Choose one of the following topics and write a paragraph or short essay about it. Use a separate sheet of paper.

1 Gender-role influences on girls in childhood

2 Reasons that there is gender inequality in the workplace

Unit **3** CONTENT QUIZ

PART 1 True/False questions (24 points)

Decide if the following statements are true (T) or false (F).

_____ **1** Negative events rather than positive ones are more likely to be reported in the media.

_____ **2** Advertising makes up the majority of the content in most daily newspapers.

_____ **3** *Propaganda* refers only to the manipulation of people's political beliefs.

_____ **4** *Internet addiction* refers to the problem of people who spend too much time on-line.

_____ **5** Misquotation only occurs in the print media, not on radio or television.

_____ **6** All research into the influence of TV violence on aggressive behavior in children shows that there is some association.

PART 2 Multiple choice questions (24 points)

Circle the best answer from the choices listed.

1 Famous or glamorous people are often used in advertisements to sell expensive products because
  a such people can easily afford to buy the products themselves.
  b this makes us think that we can be like those glamorous people if we buy the product.
  c famous people enjoy the publicity they get from doing the advertisements.
  d famous people are willing to do advertisements for free because they do not need the money.

2 Editors of newspapers are sometimes faced with ethical questions in deciding whether or not to publish a photograph. Which of the following is an ethical question?
  a Is the photograph an appropriate size for the news story?
  b Is the photograph of a famous person or a "nobody"?
  c Will it cost of lot of money to buy the photograph from the photographer?
  d Will the publication of the photograph cause harm to the people involved?

3 Paparazzi
  a use aggressive or intrusive methods to get a good photograph of a famous person.
  b are a new phenomenon that began with the invention of the digital camera.
  c only use unethical methods or illegal means to obtain photographs.
  d were made illegal after the death of Princess Diana.

4 A study of violence on television by Matthews and Ellis (1985) found that
  a television drama contained the most frequent displays of violence on television.
  b killing was most commonly shown on children's programs.
  c cartoons contained the highest levels of violence on television.
  d eighty percent of television programs contained no violence.

PART 3 Short answer questions (24 points)

Write a short answer to each of the following questions. In most cases no more than one or two sentences is required.

1 What does the term *mass media* refer to? Give examples.

2 Name three functions the media can perform in society.

3 Give two examples of how false information can be published in the media.

PART 4 One paragraph or short essay answer (28 points)

Choose one of the following topics and write a paragraph or short essay about it. Use a separate sheet of paper.

1 Strategies used in advertisements to persuade readers to buy a product

2 Concerns related to Internet communication

Unit **4** CONTENT QUIZ

PART 1 True/False questions (24 points)

Decide if the following statements are true (T) or false (F).

_____ **1** Murders are more likely to be committed against someone known to the murderer than against a stranger.

_____ **2** Murder rates in the United States increased significantly between 1991 and 1998.

_____ **3** If you do not speed because you do not want a fine, you have used an example of internal control.

_____ **4** In the "war against drugs" more money has been spent on education than on punishment.

_____ **5** It is possible to retrieve a fingerprint from human skin.

_____ **6** Many high-tech crimes that involve computers are not reported to police.

PART 2 Multiple choice questions (24 points)

Circle the best answer from the choices listed.

1 Recent crime figures in the United States show
   a an increase in the number of violent crimes committed.
   b an increase in violent crimes committed by young people.
   c that the majority of crimes are committed by young women.
   d that criminals are more likely to be employed than unemployed.

2 The use of DNA in solving crimes is an advance on using fingerprints alone because
   a everyone has different DNA.
   b DNA information can be stored in computer data banks.
   c DNA can be obtained from many sources.
   d DNA can be collected from a glass or a doorknob.

3 Rehabilitation of prisoners often fails because
   a prisoners are cut off from society and mix mainly with other criminals.
   b prisoners are not allowed to work while they are in prison.
   c it is impossible to rehabilitate someone who has committed a serious crime.
   d most prisoners feel "at home" in prison and want to stay there.

4 The majority of studies of the effects of the death penalty show that
   a the death penalty is effective in reducing the murder rate.
   b the death penalty results in increased rates of murder.
   c the death penalty does not have an effect on murder rates.
   d the death penalty results in increased numbers of arrests for murder.

PART 3 Short answer questions (24 points)

Write a short answer to each of the following questions. In most cases no more than one or two sentences is required.

1 What are *victimless crimes*? Give an example.

2 "Advances in technology, especially the extensive use of computers . . . have brought with them new kinds of crime." Give three examples of these new kinds of crime.

3 Why aren't external controls very effective in deterring "crimes of passion"?

PART 4 One paragraph or short essay answer (28 points)

Choose one of the following topics and write a paragraph or short essay about it. Use a separate sheet of paper.

1 The differences in the figures for male and female criminals, and the reasons for these differences

2 How DNA can be used to solve crimes, and some of the concerns about the use of DNA

Name _____ Date _____

Unit 5 CONTENT QUIZ

PART 1 True/False questions (24 points)

Decide if the following statements are true (T) or false (F).

_____ 1 Members of the same cultural group do not share exactly the same values and attitudes on all things.

_____ 2 Cultures only change very slowly over time.

_____ 3 The information revolution is another name for the industrial revolution.

_____ 4 Three times more people now live in urban areas than lived in them at the beginning of the 20th century.

_____ 5 The use of the automobile is contributing to global warming.

_____ 6 Making predictions about the proportion of young people to old people in future populations is part of the science of demography.

PART 2 Multiple choice questions (24 points)

Circle the best answer from the choices listed.

1 A change in the work ethic means
   a a change in the kinds of jobs that people do.
   b a change in where people work, from the office to the home.
   c a change in the hours that people work.
   d a change in people's attitude toward work.

2 Youth subcultures have become a global phenomenon because
   a many young people travel extensively around the world.
   b advances in technology have enabled young people to keep in touch with influences from other countries.
   c all young people enjoy the same music, no matter what countries they come from.
   d young people like to learn other languages and find out about other customs.

3 Fertility rates are
   a declining overall, but vary from country to country.
   b rising overall, but vary from country to country.
   c declining in some parts of the world but rising in others.
   d high and increasing in all African and Asian countries.

4 One important principle of nature is
   a that people in industrialized countries use up more than their fair share of the world's resources.
   b that people care about what belongs to them as private individuals more than they care about what belongs to them as part of the whole community.
   c that everything human beings do has an effect on the environment.
   d that human beings are continually learning how to control nature.

PART 3 Short answer questions (24 points)

Write a short answer to each of the following questions. In most cases no more than one or two sentences is required.

1 Why do some people argue that the cell phone encourages surveillance?

2 What are the three great technological revolutions that led to population surges around the world over the past million years?

3 What is Project Phoenix and what have been the results of the project so far?

PART 4 One paragraph or short essay answer (28 points)

Choose one of the following topics and write a paragraph or short essay about it. Use a separate sheet of paper.

1 Two ways that cultural change can occur

2 One problem facing our world in the future

Unit **1** CONTENT QUIZ ANSWERS

PART 1

F **1**

F **2**

T **3**

T **4**

T **5**

F **6**

PART 2

c **1**

c **2**

b **3**

a **4**

PART 3

1 Cohabitation is when an unmarried couple live together as if they were married, whereas communal living is when a group of people live together as a unit or community, sharing their skills and possessions.

2 Positive sanctions are rewards that encourage a child to repeat a behavior and negative sanctions are punishments that discourage a child from repeating the behavior. A positive sanction could be giving a child a gift, and a negative sanction could be not allowing a child to watch television.

3 Running away from a burning house is not an example of panic because this would be a perfectly sensible thing to do in this situation. Panic is an irrational response to a dangerous situation.

PART 4

1 Reference should be made to some of the following: two-career families, single-parent families, step families, cohabitation, staying single, and communal living.

2 Reference could be made to the value of the adolescent peer group, the development of subcultures, the difference between the values of the peer group and other socializing agents, and the gradual shift away from the influence of the peer group as adolescents grow older. Students could use their own experiences to illustrate ideas.

Unit 2 CONTENT QUIZ ANSWERS

PART 1

_F_ **1**

_T_ **2**

_F_ **3**

_F_ **4**

_T_ **5**

_T_ **6**

PART 2

_c_ **1**

_d_ **2**

_b_ **3**

_b_ **4**

PART 3

1 Answer should be one of the following:

- Toy stores are filled with gender-specific toys, for example, war toys for boys and domestic toys for girls.
- Even if parents give children gender-neutral toys, it is difficult to get friends and relatives to do likewise.
- Parents have to fight the gender lessons of books, the peer group, and school.

2 Men feel a loss of self-esteem when they lose their jobs because, for most men, their identity comes from their work. It is also because society expects men to earn money to support their families.

3 Answer should be two of the following reasons:

- People worry that their normal, friendly behavior could be considered sexual harassment, which may affect normal professional relationships.
- Laws and policies may deny individual rights by telling individuals how they should behave and even how they should speak.
- Women fear that laws and policies will make women seem less powerful because they will be seen as weak creatures who require special handling.
- Putting nonsexist people in management positions may be a better strategy than making laws against sexual harassment.

PART 4

1 Reference should be made to some or all of the following: parental and societal influences concerning the way girls are generally brought up; the influence of children's books, especially fairy tales; gender lessons within the school; and the influence of the media.

2 Reference should be made to some or all of the following: prejudice against women; the fact that women generally hold lower-status, lower-paying jobs, or jobs in subordinate positions to men; the fact that many women are willing to trade career advancement for some freedom to bring up their families; the fact that there are still very few women in higher management positions.

Unit 3 CONTENT QUIZ ANSWERS

PART 1

_T_ **1**

_T_ **2**

_F_ **3**

_T_ **4**

_F_ **5**

_F_ **6**

PART 2

_b_ **1**

_d_ **2**

_a_ **3**

_c_ **4**

PART 3

1 *Mass media* refers to the channels of communication that exist to reach a large public audience. Examples include television, radio, newspapers, and the Internet.

2 The answer should be that the media performs three of the following functions:

- entertainment
- education
- socialization
- important community information

- propaganda
- companionship

3 The answer should be two of the following:
- the reporter fails to check the facts
- there is a deliberate exaggeration of information
- sources are misquoted
- interviews are edited to alter questions or answers

1 The answer should include the following points: giving information about the product that is helpful to the consumer; creating an image of beauty or an idyllic lifestyle; using a famous or glamorous person so that we associate the product with fame and glamour; design features such as the use of close-up pictures of models making eye contact with the camera and the use of certain colors or playful language to attract our attention.

2 The answer should include the following points: the lack of censorship or control over what appears on the Internet; concerns about a lack of privacy in Internet communication; the misuse of the Internet in workplaces; and Internet addiction.

Unit 4 CONTENT QUIZ ANSWERS

PART 1

_T_ 1

_F_ 2

_F_ 3

_F_ 4

_T_ 5

_T_ 6

PART 2

_b_ 1

_c_ 2

_a_ 3

_c_ 4

PART 3

1 *Victimless crimes* are ones that do not involve harm to anyone other than the criminals themselves. An example would be gambling, prostitution, or drug abuse.

2 The answer should be three of the following:
- theft of money by illegally transferring money electronically
- stealing software from the Internet
- selling fake goods or setting up fake companies on the Internet to defraud people
- deliberately writing and sending viruses to damage other computers
- hacking into computer systems to steal information

3 In committing a crime of passion, the criminal may be so angry or out of control that he or she is not able to consider the consequences.

PART 4

1 The answer should mention some of the significant differences in crime figures for men and women, for example differences in the percentage of males and females arrested in the United States, and/or differences in the kinds of crimes that are characteristic of male and female criminals. The reasons for these differences include society's greater tolerance of male criminals, the social pressure on women to conform, the fact that there are fewer opportunities for women to be recruited into criminal groups, and the fact that women are socialized to be less driven than men to achieve material success.

2 The answer should mention that every person (except an identical twin) has some unique feature of his or her DNA. This means that if a sample of DNA is collected from a crime scene and matched to a suspect, it can be used as evidence that the person was present. The answer may give some examples of how DNA can be collected, and of how computer data banks can now be used to help match DNA samples. The concerns have to do with the legality of someone collecting another person's DNA without their permission, with the question of what kinds of analyses are done on the DNA, and with the question of who has access to the information.

Unit 5 CONTENT QUIZ ANSWERS

PART 1

_T_ 1
_F_ 2
_F_ 3

_F_ **4**

_T_ **5**

_T_ **6**

PART 2

_d_ **1**

_b_ **2**

_a_ **3**

_c_ **4**

PART 3

1 *Surveillance* means to keep track of someone, and the cell phone makes it easier for us to keep track of each other throughout the day, wherever we are.

2 The three great technological revolutions were
- the invention of tool making
- the invention of farming (the agricultural revolution)
- the industrial revolution

3 Project Phoenix is the most recent SETI (Search for Extra-Terrestrial Intelligence) project. It has used the most advanced equipment of any SETI project to date but has found nothing.

PART 4

1 Answers should include two of the following:
- Variation within one subgroup of a larger culture gradually spreads to other subgroups and to the broader culture. This can happen, for example, with fashions in clothes or music, as well as with attitudes and values.
- the introduction of new technologies such as computers or cell phones
- contact between different cultures that brings about exchanges of ideas or artifacts
- public or political debate about attitudes and values

2 Students could choose to focus on one of the following:
- a problem related to population, for example, declining fertility rates or increasing urbanization
- a problem related to the environment, for example, diminishing resources, global warming, or the hole in the ozone layer
- a problem related to future challenges in relation to demographic, social, or technological change